TERRORISM
From Popular Struggle
to Media Spectacle

TERRORISM
From Popular Struggle
to Media Spectacle

Gerard Chaliand

1987   London

1987

Saqi Books

**British Library
Cataloguing in Publication Data**

Chaliand, Gérard
  Terrorism : from popular struggle to
  media spectacle.
  1. Terrorism
  I. Title II. Terrorismes et guerillas.
  English
  322.4'2   HV6431
  ISBN 0-86356-168-3
  ISBN 0-86356-083-0 Pbk

**Library of Congress
Cataloguing in Publication Data**

  LC 87-9887

First published as
Terrorismes et Guérillas
by Editions Flammarion, Paris, 1985.
© Editions Flammarion, 1985.

This edition first published 1987 by
Saqi Books, 26 Westbourne Grove, London W2 5RH
and 171 First Avenue, Atlantic Highlands, NJ 07716.
© Saqi Books, 1987.

Printed in Great Britain by
Billing and Sons Ltd,
Worcester.

Contents

Abbreviations
and Acronyms

AASO	Arab Armed Struggle Organization
ANC	African National Congress (South Africa)
ASALA	Armenian Secret Army for the Liberation of Armenia
CCC	Communist Combatant Cells (Belgium)
CIA	Central Intelligence Agency (US)
CPC	Code of Criminal Procedure (West Germany)
DPIK	Democratic Party of Iranian Kurdistan
EOKA	National Organization of Cypriot Struggle
EPLF	Eritrean People's Liberation Front
ERP	People's Revolutionary Army (Argentina)
ETA	Euzkadi ta Askatasuna (Basque separatist organization)
FLN	National Liberation Front (Algeria)
Frelimo	Front for the Liberation of Mozambique
IMRO	Internal Macedonian Revolutionary Organization
IRA	Irish Republican Army
JCAG	Justice Commandos for the Armenian Genocide
LARF	Lebanese Armed Revolutionary Factions
MPLA	Popular Movement for the Liberation of Angola
NATO	North Atlantic Treaty Organization
NLF	National Liberation Front (South Vietnam)
OAS	Secret Army Organization (France)
OPEC	Organization of Petroleum Exporting Countries

PAIGC	African Party for the Independence of Guinea and Cape Verde
PDFLP	Popular Democratic Front for the Liberation of Palestine
PFLE	Popular Front for the Liberation of Eritrea
PFLP	Popular Front for the Liberation of Palestine
PLO	Palestine Liberation Organization
RNM (Renamo)	Mozambique National Resistance
SAS	Special Air Service (Britain)
SWAPO	South West Africa People's Organization
UK	United Kingdom
UN	United Nations
UNITA	National Union for the Total Independence of Angola
US	United States
USSR	Union of Soviet Socialist Republics

Preface

Over the last few decades Western military analysts have produced little that is new. Writers and intellectuals have turned their attention almost exclusively to speculation about nuclear warfare, yet even in this area they have made very few conceptual advances. Often they have been content to draw up inventories of the opposing armouries. In the past, conventional warfare was subject to detailed analysis, battles were divided up into stages, and so on, but very little thought was given to what has become the major phenomenon of our times, at least on the ground: guerrilla warfare.

Whether called revolutionary or subversive war, guerrilla warfare is now a subject of considerable importance, yet a major part of today's research concentrates on counter-insurgency, and even those works that deal with the fighting from the insurgents' viewpoint often lack objectivity. There are virtually no courses on the political and military aspects of guerrilla warfare (or indeed on terrorism), whether at military academies or university departments of war studies. Many research grants have been wasted on ambitious-sounding projects that come up with mediocre and far from operational conclusions. The phenomenon of contemporary terrorism, which is in large part propaganda terrorism, is the most violent form of psychological warfare, and it is from this angle too that it must be studied and fought against. The only general work in French devoted to the problems of guerrilla wars dates from 1958,[1] and is of limited interest.

Since the end of the Second World War guerrilla warfare has altered the map of the world. There are myriad examples: the Far East (China, Indochina); Africa (Algeria, Angola, Mozambique); Latin America (Cuba, Nicaragua); the Middle East (Israel, the Palestinians). In a world where the threat of a nuclear holocaust has so far prevented war, conflicts are generally settled by indirect strategies such as crisis management, guerrilla warfare and terrorism, and only more rarely by conventional war.

The unprecedented importance of guerrilla warfare today is due to its emergence as revolutionary war, thanks to several factors. First, one should mention the Second World War and its aftermath, which marked the end of European hegemony. Japan's initial victories in the Far East were followed by a gradual weakening of the West's imperial drive in a rapidly changing world. The second factor was the innovatory nature of Mao Zedong's concept of revolutionary war as compared to traditional guerrilla warfare — the latter being simply a series of operations by irregular forces, depending on mobility and an element of surprise, and aimed at harassing a regular army. For a long time, guerrilla forces were thought of merely as an adjunct (Clausewitz). Revolutionary war, on the other hand, is a military technique for seizing power.

Mao Zedong's innovative contribution was to graft the vanguard party onto the peasantry. The concept of the vanguard party, made up of professional revolutionaries — today a commonplace — was the creation of Lenin, whose goal was to mobilize and lead the proletariat in the seizure of power. Thanks to this new type of leadership in China, the peasantry went beyond the level of a *jacquerie*, or peasant uprising. Mao Zedong's military victory over the troops of Chiang Kai-shek in 1949 stunned the world — Stalin had not expected it any more than the American experts.

Since then, first in Indochina and subsequently in Asia (Malaya, the Philippines), Europe (Greece, Cyprus), Africa and Latin America, the techniques of revolutionary war have been applied with varying degrees of success. They have even been adopted by movements that are far from being Communist.

The national struggle most likely to succeed is that against a foreign adversary. This is particularly true if the adversary is a democratic state, since in this case a military victory is not necessary. It is enough to hold out until the adversary realizes he is unable to win militarily and tires of his intervention overseas, and a strong peace party has developed in the metropole. Victory can then be negotiated politically (Algeria and South Vietnam are two examples).

In today's world, the 'ideal' liberation war — and the one assured of maximum international support — is a war that pitches an Afro-Asian movement against the West. In a dictatorship, by contrast, whether totalitarian or not, there is no room for negotiation (Afghanistan, Salazar's Portugal).

If a social struggle in an independent country is to win, it must lead to the military defeat or the collapse of the state. Minority struggles are particularly difficult in the Third World: the very concept of autonomy is anathema to the state (which fears that the minority may secede), and most Afro-Asian countries will only aid such movements if by doing so they also weaken a neighbouring state.

The role of terrorism has become increasingly important in political affairs over the last fifteen years or so. The phenomenon in itself is not new and goes back to tyrannicide, but today's terrorism is of a particular kind. It has virtually nothing in common with the conventional terrorism long used by political movements with a specialist armed wing, such as Irgun and the Stern Gang within the framework of the Zionist movement, for example.

Terrorism's growing impact can be attributed almost exclusively to the development of the media, and above all to the televised image combined with propaganda-type, often transnational terrorism in which the participants frequently represent no one but themselves. When this type of propaganda terrorism is used by a political movement of some size, it becomes a substitute for guerrilla warfare (the Irish Republican Army (IRA), the Palestinians).

Both guerrilla warfare and terrorism are the weapon of the weak against the strong. As techniques, they are neither of the Right nor of the Left. For the last fifteen years or so, propaganda terrorism has been used mainly as a weapon of psychological warfare. It may be useful here to distinguish between different types of terrorism. First, there are terrorist movements which have no mass base and are doomed to failure because of their blinkered ideological stance; they are found mainly in the industrialized countries (the Weathermen in the United States, the Baader-Meinhof group in West Germany, the Red Brigades in Italy). Such movements are distinct from groups with a degree of social depth (the IRA in Northern Ireland, the Basque ETA fighting for autonomy, the Palestinians). The third category is state terrorism (whether for domestic or external use), not forgetting the state's use of torture.

As an independent participant-observer, I have devoted a considerable part of my life to national liberation movements in Africa, Latin America, the Middle East and South-East Asia. I have never worked for an institution, nor have I enjoyed the support — whether direct or indirect — that French and US researchers receive from the French state and private American foundations. Though I have received several invitations from liberation movements, I have generally financed my field trips myself. A dozen years spent on three continents, including some eighteen months in areas of revolutionary or guerrilla warfare, have gradually enabled me to understand the complex political and strategic problems involved.

Nothing in particular destined me more than others of my generation, also engaged in anti-colonial struggles, to make the series of choices that took me to Guinea-Bissau in 1964 and 1966 with Amilcar Cabral; to North Vietnam during the American bombardments in 1967, when I looked into the organization of villages in the Red River delta; to the Colombian provinces of Tolima and Huila in 1968; to Jordan and Lebanon from 1969 to 1970 with Fatah, the Popular Front for the Liberation of Palestine (PFLP) and the Popular Democratic Front for the Liberation of Palestine (PDFLP); to Eritrea in 1977; to Iranian Kurdistan in 1980; and three times to Afghanistan in 1980 and 1982. Nothing except the lure of action, a familiarity with nature, a taste for walking and the fact of liking the atmosphere of war. For those who are content with the bare essentials of life — and on condition they come out unscathed — the precariousness of war gives a special value to every moment, to every human contact. It is not that I find guerrilla war fascinating: we are only fascinated by what we know from afar. It has many different facets, though observers tend to treat it as a series of hiking expeditions. Its real interest lies elsewhere, however: in the study of how a society reacts in order to face a situation of violent crisis; and in the political and strategic intelligence of a leadership or cadres who are able to seize on the adversary's vulnerable points, get ordinary people involved and create the conditions for sustained action. In this respect, I learned a great deal from Amilcar Cabral, and still more from the Vietnamese: but very little elsewhere. I found the same qualities in the fighters of the Eritrean People's Liberation Front (EPLF) as in the Vietnamese. A visitor enjoys a privileged status; I have almost always been received as a friend, and at the very least with kindness.

As far as the risks are concerned, these vary enormously from one guerrilla war to another, and from one phase of the struggle to the next. They are, for example, very slight in Afghanistan because there is as yet no systematic counter-insurgency. Chance, of course, is ever present, and it is a young Afghan *mujahid* that I have to thank for having prevented me from stepping on a Soviet anti-personnel mine in October 1980. At the other extreme, the risks were very great in Guinea-Bissau, where we were under constant bombardment (the baptism of fire is above all a shock to the ears), twice at such close range that we lost some of our travelling companions. We were also chased by airborne units. During the intense bombing of North Vietnam by American B52s, both soldiers and civilians were killed near the foxhole where I was sheltering in a village in Thai Binh province in November 1967. The Latin American guerrilla movements of the 1960s were dangerous in a different way because of their irresponsibility and lack of organization.

Apart from parasite-borne diseases or fevers contracted in tropical areas (the toughest guerrillas are those in the tropical forests in the rainy season), the actual risks are somewhat limited. Moreover, the participant-observer only needs to use weapons if he has to break out of an encirclement where he and his comrades have become sitting ducks.

As the *Strategic Atlas*[2] has shown, the fact that globes tended to put Europe at the centre of the world was no more than the remnant of a bygone era. At a time when Europe dominated the world, this pictorial convention was the expression of a *de facto* situation. Yet for several decades it had been no more than a habit reflecting intellectual laziness. The same can be said of strategic analysts, who, apart from a few nuclear theoreticians, go round in circles without learning anything from today's armed struggles. The pattern of war has changed: there are relatively few conventional wars, but a considerable number of guerrilla wars and the development of terrorist-type actions. With guerrilla warfare, rapid deployment operations, urban fighting, terrorism and psychological warfare, indirect strategies are increasingly on the agenda; yet the experiences of yesterday have not always been properly assimilated nor has the knowledge gained been adapted to the innovations of today. It is these questions that this short work seeks to answer.

1
The Tool-Box

During the era of colonial expansion, a relatively small number of European troops managed to conquer and control most of Asia and Africa. Less than a century later, guerrillas, again often in small numbers, were able to hold Western armies in check. How had this change come about?

The conquests can, of course, largely be explained by technological advances: the initial successes were made possible by the steamer, telecommunications, the monopoly of the machine-gun and new prophylactics against malaria. So has the West now lost this technological superiority? Not necessarily: unless a guerrilla movement (or revolutionary war) wants to work towards a frontal assault as at Dien Bien Phu, it does not need to attain the adversary's overall level of weaponry.

This is not the basic issue, however. It was not technological superiority that constituted the essence of Europe's supremacy in the nineteenth century. The subjugation of the colonized peoples was due to the Whites' *conceptual* superiority at this particular point in history. With the exception of Japan, it took the colonized and semi-colonized peoples two or three generations to make up much of this gap: that is, to turn the Europeans' own weapons and conceptual equipment against them.

The West's colonial ambitions covered a vast geographical

area. Russian imperialism pushed towards the Caucasus, Central Asia, Chinese Turkestan and Manchuria; the United States towards Mexico (as well as Puerto Rico, the Philippines, and so on); and Europe towards Asia and Africa. China itself was forced to open up.

Colonialism has left an ambiguous legacy. When seen within a historical context, its oppressive and exploitative side must be weighed against the introduction of the basic features of modernity. The intellectual and scientific revolution that took shape during the Enlightenment turned Europe upside down, and some of its conceptual innovations — notably the modern concept of nationalism — were to spread worldwide.

The 'civilizing mission' was obviously not the real goal of colonial expansion. All societies are hypocritical, with the possible exception of the classical despotic societies, which needed no justification other than the legitimacy of force. The gap between words, statements, programmes and aims on the one hand, and facts on the other, is everywhere glaringly apparent (though far less pronounced in democratic societies).

The excesses of the colonial period are well known: slavery and the slave trade, the decimation of Indian populations (north as well as south of the Rio Grande, as far as Argentina), the disintegration of the populations of the South Pacific, the atrocities committed in China (1840) and South-West Africa (1905-07).

It is worth remembering that even in what is considered the world's most democratic country, the United States, slavery was abolished little more than a century ago and the discriminatory laws against Blacks only in 1954, while equal political rights were gained in the early 1960s, scarcely more than twenty years ago.

As for Asian and African societies, they were ruled by traditional rulers and chiefs who were despotic and all-powerful and enjoyed a monopoly of political power.[1] Their subjects busied themselves with their own affairs. Slavery was the norm. The Ottoman and Manchu empires, the Indian principalities and the Malayan sultanates were all corrupt, oppressive and decadent. The 'communalism' of African villages involved superstition, tribal wars and slavery.

When, in the second half of the nineteenth century, Europe swooped down on Africa and Asia, even the most advanced of these societies (and particularly those with a long state tradition) were faced with a model that was conceptually incomprehensible. Their initial reaction was an outright xenophobic rejection and a withdrawal into traditional, notably religious, values. In all societies with a state tradition the reaction was the same.

In 1840 China was defeated by Britain in the Opium war. Though forced to open its doors, China initially retained a confidence in the superiority of its own culture. As one humiliation followed another in the face of European arms, however, the mandarins became increasingly worried at the country's obvious weakness. Young Chinese were sent to study science in Europe and the United States, in the belief that the West's superiority lay in its advanced science and technology.

Farther west, both Muhammad Ali (in Egypt) and the Ottoman empire tried to assimilate only the West's military and technical prowess while continuing to think within a traditional framework — such efforts proved fruitless.

It gradually became apparent that, in order to preserve one's identity, it was necessary not only to retain solid links with the past, but also to acquire some mastery of the concepts, ideas and institutions that had helped shape the modern West.

Only Japan (whose throne was occupied by a home-grown dynasty) was in a position to respond to the challenge of the White Peril. It already enjoyed the advantages of ethnic and social cohesion and a certain insularity. By means of a revolution from the top by second-ranking samurais, the country now moved quickly to introduce the necessary changes. It was an elitist revolution that kept the people subjected, but it nevertheless raised the question of why the West was superior. In 1932, however, the first hesitant steps towards democracy were swept aside in the wake of the world economic crisis and the rise of ultra-nationalism. It was the defeat of 1945, the American occupation and the constitution imposed by MacArthur[2] that finally established democracy.

In 1894 China suffered the great shock of being defeated by Japan. For the educated Chinese it was a traumatic experience. To be defeated by Britain or France (as in 1884) was one thing: to be defeated by Japan was a disaster. The Chinese needed urgently to pull themselves together. All previous responses seemed inadequate. Some people tried to work out a 'true' Confucianism, one not systematically turned towards the past but open to progress. The most original conceptual breakthrough was that of Yen Fu, who, in 1895, barely a year after the disaster, sought in his four 'manifestos' to discover the key to the West's power. Yen Fu observed that the monarchy was powerless against the foreigner and despotic in its dealings with the people. The sclerotic administration was the inevitable consequence of having a corrupt mandarinate that considered itself all-knowing, while being totally ignorant of the outside world. Yen Fu introduced the idea of perpetual progress, whose driving force is struggle, in place of the cyclical conception that gives pride of place to the cult of the past.

Wherever the move towards modernity was seen as something other than the mere absorption of military or scientific techniques, it was fraught with difficulties. The Ottoman empire, for example (which only survived after 1878 thanks to Anglo-Russian rivalry), never succeeded in making the transition. The adoption of German military techniques was not enough to ensure recovery. The Young Turk revolution was the direct result of the intellectual crisis, yet despite its desire for modernization, it was unable to transform the empire or work out a viable new ideology — after hesitating between Ottomanism (an empire of Muslims) and Pan-Turanianism (an empire for all Turks as far as Central Asia). It was left to Mustafa Kemal Atatürk to save the country from disaster by creating modern Turkey on the European model of the nation-state.

The most complex problem was how to assimilate, in the space of a few generations, the conceptual core elaborated by Europe towards the end of the eighteenth century and during the nineteenth. Here were totally new revolutionary ideas[3] that were difficult to put into practice without the necessary pre-conditions. It took the local elites in the colonial and semi-colonial societies half a century to discover the tool-box containing the instruments giving access to the West's superiority and power.

What was it that had to be discovered? First came nationalism, a totally new idea. Imperial arrogance and racial discrimination were to help nationalism on its way: they lay at the root of the sense of humiliation experienced by the colonial and semi-colonial peoples.

> The Third World is not a single whole. It is made up of very different cultures at various levels of technical, economic and cultural development. But over the last 150 years, at different points in the evolution of these peoples and placed in the novel circumstances of a shared situation of humiliation and subjugation before a single ruler — the European-American West — the same rupture occurred throughout the Third World. I suggest calling it the end of resignation...
>
> But at the same time as Europe was grinding down peoples and continents with its iron heel, it was revealing another facet. Although it was the hated land of the oppressor, it also came to be seen as a model of liberation, even as several models. To the elites, hopelessly cowed before despotism, the West provided a model of government in

which the interests and aspirations of all the subjects could have an institutionalized voice. To all those sunk for long centuries in conformist approval, it gave an example of a world where everything was perpetually being questioned. As this aspect of the Western world was revealed, people came to realize that it was possible to fight for a better state and a better society. Hope was rekindled.

People started to analyse their situation of oppression and humiliation. At first they did so within the traditional structures of thought. Was not the West's success due to the religion it so often used as its banner? Should not greater efforts be made to fight this religion, or at least to update one's own religion in its image or perhaps borrow its methods? Some people went so far as to take over certain of its dogmas, to create 'colonial heresies', syncretistic religious movements. Subsequently, they began to ask whether the analysis should not be a political one. Was it not better to use the West's methods of political struggle and adopt its forms of government? At all events, nationalism — the great ideology of nineteenth-century Europe — was adopted. It provided a perfectly adequate ideological framework for the great revolt against Europe, which was preparing for war.[4]

Contrary to received ideas in the schools of the French Third and Fourth Republics, modern nationalism is a very recent idea.[5] The idea that a nation has 'natural rights' and that the nation legitimizes the state was first formulated as a proposition with universal validity during the French revolution.[6] This revolutionary idea was to spread throughout Europe during the course of the nineteenth century. The revolution meant that if the citizens (not the subjects) of a state no longer approve of the political organization of their society, they have the right and the power to replace it with a better system. The view that men possess 'natural rights', that they can be born with equal rights, was particularly new.

Even today this idea, though self-evident in the West, is seen as absurd by many societies with a despotic tradition. On the contrary, it is the notion that *inequality* is in the natural order of things that appears obvious in traditional societies.

Napoleon's armies helped to spread the novel ideas of the French revolution to the four corners of Europe, where the creation of the nation-state gradually became the accepted goal. The national awakening of the German elites occurred after the Prussian disaster at Jena in 1806. The generation of Herder, Fichte, Gneisenau, Scharnhorst and Clausewitz found in Napoleon not only an enemy but also an example to be followed.

The Congress of Vienna in 1815 denied the new legitimacy of the nation. A century later, the Austrian empire was to die as a result of this refusal.

Once the French revolution had introduced the challenge of the 'nation in arms', Europe's non-democratic regimes were faced with a dilemma: how to enjoy popular support and yet retain their monopoly of power and privilege. In Russia the despotic tradition allowed this sort of dilemma to be postponed until the First World War. Elsewhere, the elites wanted to benefit from the national democratic revolution without having to pay the price of a revolution.

Independence and national unity were the West's central themes during the nineteenth century. The models were patriots struggling for their rights and their peoples — men such as Kossuth and Garibaldi. As for the ideas, they were drawn at random from Rousseau, Burke, Fichte, Mazzini.

The idea of the nation was introduced into the most advanced societies of Asia (elsewhere in the Third World, only Egypt possessed elites of a comparable level) at the turn of the century. For the few elites who had come to appreciate the historical backwardness of their societies, it posed a difficult question: how to elicit national consciousness.

In addition to nationalism and the nation-state, the elites

of Asian and then African societies had to assimilate various other ideas before they could turn them against Europe and thus liberate themselves. The Chinese revolution that put an end to the Manchu dynasty in 1910 and the Young Turk revolution of 1908 had provided a republican model, for example. Another new idea was that of the party: allegiance no longer went automatically to the ruler or his representative, but to the party whose programme expressed the aspirations of both the elites and (at least in theory) the people (examples were the Indian National Congress and the Egyptian Wafd).

The initial reaction was one of rejection, subsequently translated into a withdrawal into religious ideology or traditional morality. Among certain urbanized, well-off and partly Westernized social layers throughout the Afro-Asian world, this was followed by a stage of acceptance of Western superiority accompanied by a self-inflicted sense of humiliation. A fraction of the new elites was ashamed at the low level and backwardness of their own masses. But this stage did not last long. Other more radical nationalist elements appeared and, in the name of national identity and dignity, took up the struggle once more.

Meanwhile, the colonial system had broken up the traditional economy, introduced private ownership of land where it had previously not existed and raised up new social groups.

The era of the great traditional rebellions such as the Boxer rebellion of 1898-1900 or the Indian rebellion of 1857 (the 'Indian mutiny') was over. Another generation had appeared on the scene, that of the Sun Yat-sens in China and the Gandhis in India. It was the time of the First World War. Soon the elites that had taken over were almost all men with a thorough knowledge of the ideas and workings of the West.

It was the assimilation of this mental equipment that made it possible to achieve national liberation, recover a sense of identity and begin the stage of nation-building. Europe thus diffused, willy-nilly, its main ideas: the nation-state, and the notion that anything less than self-government is servitude. Great societies with a state tradition, such as China, could no longer afford to ignore or underestimate the new barbarians; it was not possible, as in Islam, to cling to a religious ideology and wait for the storm to blow over.

After the First World War there were only marginal increases in the area under colonial domination: the British and French mandates in the Middle East in 1920; Italy's colonization of Libya from 1922 to 1932 and, in 1935, of Ethiopia; the expansion of the Japanese empire in 1937.

In 1918 the American president Woodrow Wilson proclaimed the right to self-determination. This principle, though supposedly universal, was applied only to Central Europe — and Armenia. It was at this time that the dismemberment of the Habsburg empire led to the creation of nation-states such as Czechoslovakia, Yugoslavia and Poland, all to some extent burdened with minority problems. At the Paris Peace Conference, colonial problems (with the exception of the mandates) played an insignificant role.

Until the beginning of the century, Darwinian theories had appeared to provide a scientific justification for the superiority of Whites — this superiority was in the order of things; it was not only obvious but theoretically and morally justified. Wilson envisaged that the grievances of the colonized peoples would be taken into account; no more. Moreover, in spite of the few great names who raised their lonely voices against servitude (today recognized as the founding fathers of modern nationalism), the colonized peoples themselves were neither conscious nor, *a fortiori*, mobilized. The immediate post-war period saw only the very first manifestations of what, a quarter of a century later (after a new world war), was to become a clamorous freedom movement.

The Baku Congress of 1920 was not the result of an Asian initiative, but of one by Russian Bolsheviks. Faced with a desperate crisis and growing threats on all sides, and thanks to an ancient state and military tradition, only Atatürk was able to free Turkey from foreign domination in 1922. (Ibn Saud was shortly to follow his example.)

In the aftermath of the First World War, the promulgation of the principle of the right to self-determination had no immediate impact on the development of nationalism among the colonized peoples. This indicates the backwardness of the overwhelming majority of the colonized elites at the time.

The principle of nations being able freely to determine their fate was proclaimed simultaneously by both the liberal American Woodrow Wilson and the Russian Bolshevik Lenin. Indeed, the new Soviet regime used this principle to incite the colonized peoples to shake off the yoke of imperialism. Although Communist Parties made a timid appearance here and there,[7] the Baku Congress, at which the majority of those present were Turkish-speakers, produced no significant results. It had taken place too early in the century.

The application of the principle of self-determination depended entirely on those elites and groups ready to make use of it. At first, the elites were very small and complex-ridden, but gradually the seditious ideas circulated and took shape.

Following the First World War, there was a wave of colonial revolts, all on a modest scale. No longer part of the initial stage of the war to resist conquest, they were the start of a challenge to the colonial order. The Concessions in China were no longer accepted without question; in 1919 King Amanullah of Afghanistan freed his country of the last vestiges of British control (those which regulated the country's external relations); in Morocco the Rif war lasted from 1925 to 1927; there were armed uprisings in Burma, in Indonesia (1926-27), in Vietnam (1930), and in Syria against the French mandate. Apart from sporadic terrorist attacks, India had a completely new type of movement, headed by Gandhi and the Indian National Congress. While Britain acted with restraint and tried to live up to its liberal ideals, Gandhi, a remarkable tactician of non-violence, applied political pressure and gradually mobilized the Indian masses to the point of near-unanimity.

The end of the war signalled the birth of the nationalist idea which was to come of age only after 1945. The spread of ideas may seem slow compared to the legitimate impatience of small groups of vanguard activists. Over a relatively brief historical time-span, however, it can be seen as rapid. One should not forget the initial level of consciousness of the masses: they were mobilized by a series of new events and slogans to the point of risking the harshest repression.

When up against the tremendous impact of the West, the colonized or semi-colonized societies faced a dilemma: how to redefine themselves and their culture. For China, the process was relatively easy: it had a long cultural heritage, and only a small part of the country had been occupied. Throughout its long history, China had hardly ever had problems of identity, shielded as it was by an underlying sense of superiority. The process of recovery was more complicated for a country like India — occupied, divided between Hindus and Muslims, and representing more a civilization than a state. And it was still more difficult for the Arab societies, where a recourse to religion did not always make up for the feeling of humiliation born of a glorious past. The problems were even more complex for Africans, torn as they were between Pan-Africanism, negritude, and traditions that were scarcely adapted to the needs of modern times.

This past, or fragments of it, were moreover restored to the colonized world by the West and that currently much-criticized field of study, Orientalism. Whatever its 'colonialist' aspects, Orientalism gave back to the societies of Asia large chunks of a past that had sometimes been forgotten and often misunderstood. Western Europe had already enabled the Ottomanized Greeks to rediscover classical Greece.

The rejection of the West (whose imperial arrogance was

a constant humiliation) was the work of the new urban elites. These elites were not only the people most exposed to racism; they were also the best equipped to deal with it since they had, at least in part, understood Western concepts and ideas. In their everyday life they felt the inherent sense of inferiority due to the colonial situation; they were always, to some extent, second-class citizens. All the movements that spread the ideas of modern nationalism[8] were born in the towns. Traditional peasant agitation was altogether different. It was caused by local grievances that, when felt to be intolerable, led to sudden spontaneous revolts. They were also revolts to preserve the traditional way of life when faced with attacks from outside. But at no time did the peasantry have a general vision of a society, nor did it ever awaken a nationwide consciousness; the homeland remained regionalized. The aspirations and goals pursued by a handful of vanguard nationalists concerned the peasantry only slightly, if at all.

The social layers that were to lead the national movements were not the traditional local rulers, who had all been defeated and/or were collaborators. They were not the Indian princes or the majority of mandarins descended from the Manchu dynasty's empire, nor were they the Malay sultans or the African chiefs. There were only two exceptions: Morocco and Uganda (Buganda).

The backbone of the national movement was provided by the urban petty bourgeoisie, or at least a fraction of it. This is not to say that the leaders did not sometimes belong to the better-off social layers. Indeed, the distinguishing feature of such leaders was almost always that they had studied in or known the West, or had in some way been marked by it (the most notable exception being Mao Zedong).[9]

In contrast, the countries that retained their traditional elites were those that had not been colonized: Yemen, Ethiopia, Afghanistan. In Siam, the aristocracy retained power. In Persia, Reza Shah, installed by the British, succeeded in the inter-war period in putting down the tribes but not the aristocracy or the landowners.

Japan's victory in the Russo-Japanese war in 1904 had been an important landmark in East Asia. It had moreover brought students to Japan from many countries, including China, all fascinated by the prospect of learning how an Asian country had been able to defeat a European power. Yet it was not possible to follow the Japanese example. The power of the West remained intact until the Second World War — after all, Tsarist Russia was a backward country, often perceived as 'semi-Asiatic'. However well organized the insurgencies between the world wars (and some, such as that of Abd al-Krim in Morocco from 1925 to 1927, were truly remarkable), all were crushed. With few exceptions, these colonial wars, conducted by professional soldiers, had the support of European public opinion. The validity of the 'civilizing mission' was never questioned. Colonialism was part of the natural order. (The great colonial exhibition in Paris was held in 1931.)

In fact, none of the great colonial powers was seriously worried before the Japanese invasion of East Asia. The Japanese victories over the Americans in the Philippines, the Dutch in Indonesia, the French in Indochina and the British in Malaya had a considerable impact. They showed that it was possible to overthrow the colonial order, that the Whites could be defeated. Since Japan's population was not large enough to occupy both China and all the countries from which the Whites had withdrawn, the colonized peoples were suddenly presented with an opportunity hitherto denied to them. In Indochina and Indonesia, the interval between Japan's surrender and the arrival of the Allied forces enabled the national liberation movements to consolidate their forces before the French and the Dutch returned.

During the Second World War there was an extremely active, if non-violent, anti-colonialist current in India. It culminated in the 'Quit India' campaign of 1942, which led to Gandhi's being imprisoned and the Congress Party being outlawed. But the break with the colonial past was definitive and the end of the war simply confirmed it.

After a war which had left Europe exhausted and marked the final end of its hegemony, barely ten years separate us from the Bandung Conference, a symbolic moment in the emancipation and political independence of Asia and, before long, Africa.

Unlike the League of Nations, which had been set up at the end of the First World War, the United Nations Charter explicitly mentioned the principle of self-determination. As we have seen, the principle had already been formulated by Woodrow Wilson and Lenin, but the effects for the colonized world had been nil. Theoretically no one is opposed to the principle of self-determination, i.e. the right of a people to be in charge of its own affairs. But it is impossible to put it into practice if a state opposes it. This is true both for a colony and for a minority that wishes to secede.

The principle is, in fact, more complex than it might appear. The Enlightenment proclaimed that governments must govern with the consent of the governed; the nineteenth century added that the government must represent the nation. Consequently, a nation has the right to a state. Thus, after the First World War states without a national base[10] were considered illegitimate.

The nineteenth century saw a gradual shift from the idea that individuals should freely establish a government to rule them to that of nations having a 'natural right' to create their own state. This was in fact the same right to self-determination that, since the time of the French revolution, had been expressed in different guises: European nationalism, Wilsonian self-determination, Asian and African decolonization, minority ethno-nationalism, and so on.

The appearance of modern nationalism not only marked the break (at least for the West) with an order based on 'divine right' and its replacement by the 'natural rights' of individuals or nations. It also marked the shift from a world where the referent was essentially religious[11] to one in which it was almost always national. In Europe the religious factor became progressively less important from the time that nationalism and national wars replaced wars of religion. In Islam, however, religion remained of fundamental importance, not only because Islam was the ideology of resistance during the colonial period, but also because it is 'both religion and state' (*dar wa dawla*).

The international community's recognition of self-determination as a basic human right spurred on the decolonization process in Asia and Africa. Though the idea was not new, the spirit of the times had changed. New elites had sprung up in the colonial countries and the era of subjugation and the ensuing inferiority complex was over: these elites no longer tolerated government by foreigners.[12] The inter-war period had favoured the notion that the colonial situation should be improved and reforms introduced; this approach was now abandoned. The Second World War, during which the Allies had fought in the name of liberty — and in which the Japanese had shown that Whites could be defeated — brought an awareness that independence could be achieved. The time was ripe in Asia, to be followed some fifteen years later by Africa. White domination must be eradicated. As for the nation-state, it was the only model, the sole tool (whether or not it suited a country's ethnic and religious composition), that could replace colonial domination. Indeed, the very principle of self-determination itself was based on the assumption that the state and the nation should coincide.

When in 1945 at San Francisco the United Nations decreed 'respect for the principle of equal rights and the self-determination of peoples', was this a right or merely a principle that should be respected? In any event, the right to secession was excluded.[13]

In 1952 the UN adopted a resolution on self-determination: but the right to self-determination has no place whatsoever in international law. The right to dispose of the national territory is an attribute of the sovereignty of each state. In practice, the right to self-determination is either left to the goodwill of the dominant power or is the result of a resort to force. It might even be seen as part of a tradition that goes back to the Enlightenment: the right to rebel against a government seen as illegitimate in that it does not respond, or no longer responds, to the aspirations of the governed.

In order to escape from European domination, the Asian and African liberation movements had to assimilate the ideas and concepts of modern Europe, beginning with nationalism. Victory was only possible through attending the school of Europe. The dream of seeing the proclamation of a nation-state was also a European model.

Two problems arose here. First, the state structure marked out by the colonizer (especially in Africa) had scant historical basis and coincided only accidentally with a more or less homogeneous ethnic group. Is the principle of self-determination applicable only to majorities? In the Afro-Asian world the creation of nation-states has almost universally led to minorities being discriminated against or oppressed.

The second problem is that the essence of the West's contribution in modern times — democracy and a respect for human rights, at least within the nation — has not been assimilated. Very few Asian, African and Latin American states operate anything approaching democracy as understood in the West. In the inter-war years the elites of the colonies and mandated territories saw parliamentary rule as an institution symbolizing one of the attributes of modernity. Yet the institution has brusquely been brushed aside by dictatorships intent on state-building. In this respect there has actually been a regression in the aspirations of the African and Asian elites. It often seems more difficult to put freedom into practice than to endure tyranny.[14] Institutions that guarantee freedoms are scornfully rejected on the pretext that the masses are not interested in them.

It is true that the pre-conditions were cruelly lacking in societies whose virtually sole experience of the state had been classical despotism followed by colonial domination. But the fault does not lie exclusively with colonialism, as is too often claimed. It is the elites — if the word is not too strong in some cases — who have seized power and now exercise it in a cynical and uneducated way.

The lack of a democratic tradition is undoubtedly a handicap, as are backwardness and poor economic conditions. Yet such handicaps are perhaps less important than the lack of a critical tradition. In these countries, the world is perceived as basically hierarchical and inegalitarian. This is what makes possible the despotism of the new elites, and the rigid social stratification in which independence has ultimately benefited only a few narrow strata. Contrary to the American myth of freedom and equal opportunity for all in a country where, in principle, everything is possible, traditional societies and the regimes they have produced (whatever their stated ideologies) neither encourage people to fight authority nor lead to greater social mobility.

In a situation of classical despotism, such as the Ottoman empire, authority was beyond the reach of the subjects. People might complain (discreetly) about the regime's impassivity, as one might complain about fate, but authority was unchangeable. Inevitably, many of its features persist to the present day in the style of republican semi-democracy created by Atatürk.

History has witnessed innumerable, notably peasant revolts (virtually always put down) that arose spontaneously from a situation felt to be intolerable. But it never occurred to the peasants (nor could it have done) that they might have rights. All the concepts and ideas mentioned above, and produced by the West not long ago, are in fact extremely novel. Many elites, or pseudo-elites, in Asia, Africa — and Latin America — are far from having absorbed the idea that men (and women) are equal before the law. For some ruling strata, the concept is even grotesque. Force is still the sole measure of relations between the state and its subjects (now called citizens, though there are none of the attributes of the dignity and rights of the citizen, nor is there any conception of a society based on civic rights).

It is also true that once the masses have been mobilized in a mood of nationalist, religious or revolutionary fervour, they seem more at ease with a government that tells them what to do than with the exercise of freedom of choice. Apathy and passivity doubtless exist. But they are due in part to the mediocrity and complacency, not to say betrayal, of the educated layers. Democracy, or more precisely minimal democracy, remains a fundamental issue for most Afro-Asian countries, and a good number of those in Latin America. It cannot be ignored indefinitely, whatever the ideology of the regime. This by no means implies that tyranny, despotism and great outbursts of collective fervour, or indeed totalitarianism, have gone for ever.

2
Guerrilla Warfare

The origin of the term *guerrilla* ('small war') dates back to 1807-12 and the Spanish uprising against the Napoleonic occupation. As a form of combat, guerrilla warfare has existed since time immemorial, but whereas many treatises — from China to Greece by way of Rome and Byzantium — had dealt with the art of conventional war, it was not until the beginning of the nineteenth century that the first treatises on guerrilla warfare were published, mainly in French and German. No one could be unaware of the scale of the bloodletting inflicted on Napoleon's armies; indeed, for some people its implications posed a problem. Although of minor significance compared to Spain, three other events — the Vendée, the Tyrol (the uprising against the Napoleonic troops) and the partisan war in Russia — were to increase the interest in guerrilla warfare.

Although the importance of Wellington's regular armies must not be underestimated, the Spanish guerrillas are credited with eliminating 400–500,000 French soldiers from the fighting. This figure is much higher than that during all the campaigns against Prussia and Austria, and almost as high as that in Russia. The role of the Russian partisans in 1812 was less significant, though they managed to increase Napoleon's supply problems and decimate the rear.

What explains this sudden increase in the number of

guerrilla wars and their relative success at this particular point in history? It cannot be attributed to modern nationalism, an ideology that was yet to be absorbed in Spain and Russia. Germany itself had a mere handful of nationalists. It was peasants who were fighting, in both the Tyrol and Spain, and though their struggle had an element of patriotism, it was principally in defence of their means of existence.

As Camille Rougeron has pointed out, 'the two great changes that made modern armies so vulnerable to guerrilla tactics were the increased use of military hardware and the massive growth in the numbers of troops deployed'.[1] The French revolution introduced the *levée en masse* and troops that had previously lived on their supplies began to live off the country (something that was quite possible in relatively rich countries like Italy or those of Central Europe, but more difficult in Spain and Russia).[2]

The French had more hardware than their adversaries (their artillery was twice the size) and having done away with food convoys, their troops gained greater mobility and were less tied down defending their lines of communication. But while this dependence on local supplies was not a problem in wealthy countries, it proved a handicap in Spain, where the peasants refused to sell their produce or allow the little they had to be seized, and in Russia, where in winter there was nothing left. Clausewitz, who was following operations from the Russian side, provided irrefutable proof of Napoleon's lack of foresight in preparing for an expedition; if supplies had been stockpiled in towns during the advance, it would have saved the Grand Army on its retreat.[3]

Le Mière de Corvey's book, *Des partisans et des corps irreguliers*, was a major contribution to the theory of guerrilla warfare:

> The aim of partisan groups is always to have a large enough force to worry the enemy, to be able to move it about wherever needed to harass him relentlessly, to wear him

down gradually, to block his supplies, to destroy and make off with his convoys, to seize his dispatches, to intercept his communications and to surprise any isolated stragglers they should chance on. When properly waged under a skilful leader, this war will strike terror in the enemy: he can hold the towns, but as he must use roads to communicate from one to another, he will be attacked on the roads; he will have to fight for every ravine; he will no longer dare let out a single unescorted waggon; he will wear out his troops, be unable to recruit more and gradually be destroyed, without ever having suffered any one major loss.[4]

With the exception of Italy (Garibaldi, 1860) and Poland (1830-31, 1863-64),[5] guerrilla warfare ceased to play a significant role in Europe after 1815. It was a time of urban uprisings, such as those of 1830, 1848 and 1871. Moreover revolutionary political thinkers of the time did not stress the peasantry, seen as conservative and backward, but the proletariat.

From the conquest of Algeria in 1830 down to the First World War, when the whole colonial world was 'pacified', guerrilla warfare occurred essentially in Asia and Africa. The characteristic feature of these guerrilla wars — whether it was the long resistance to the Russian advance into the Caucasus or Central Asia, or the struggle against the British in India, Burma[6] and Africa, the Dutch in Java, the Americans in the Philippines (1898-1901) and the French in Indochina and West Africa — is that they were, without exception, ultimately defeated.

The only European defeat at this time was in the context of a conventional war: the Italian disaster at the battle of Adowa against the Ethiopians in 1896.

Westerners — Europeans — triumphed everywhere, thanks to superior weaponry (the machine-gun was now proving to be of decisive importance). Every so often the odd battle was lost, of course: in 1879, for example, the Zulus trounced the British regiments at Isandlwana. It took some thirty years for British and French forces to put down the various resistance movements in West Africa.

There were some particularly hard-fought wars: in Algeria against Abd al–Kader (1830–47); in South Africa against the Zulus; in South-West Africa (Morenga); in the Sudan against the Mahdists (1885-98), a messianic movement; in the North-West Frontier against the Pathans (1897-98); in the Philippines (1899-1901); in Somalia against Mohammed Abdille Hassan, who resisted the British for twenty years (1899-1920). The fierce resistance movements in both Central Asia and the Caucasus (notably that of Shaikh Shamil in Azerbaijan) lasted several decades (1836-59). At the beginning of the Rif war, Abd al–Krim succeeded in inflicting a national disaster on the Spanish at Anual in 1921.[7] In the Libyan province of Cyrenaica, Omar Mukhtar held out against the Italians for ten years (1922-32).

René Pélissier[8] has counted over 100 uprisings in Angola between 1840 and 1930 and in Mozambique between 1840 and 1918. Despite their unequal weapons, these resistance movements won the occasional major battle (Gatling, 1862; Maxim, 1884), yet none of them emerged victorious. In the end, they were all put down. Not only were they up against an adversary enjoying undeniable military superiority; the wars were waged by professional soldiers backed by a state and supported by a public convinced of the wars' validity and with no qualms as to the purpose of the colonial mission.

For Europe, and for Western strategists, guerrilla warfare rightly remained a marginal phenomenon. The great military theoreticians of the period 1860-1930 were interested in conventional warfare, or in improved sea power. The Crimean war, Sadowa, Sedan, the First World War, left little place for guerrilla warfare, though one might perhaps mention the activities of the *francs-tireurs* in the 1870 war and of Lawrence of Arabia during the First World War.

Guerrilla struggles continued nevertheless: the Armenian *fedayeen* movement from 1894 to 1908; the Macedonian movement (Internal Macedonian Revolutionary Organization (IMRO) from 1919 to 1934, with Todor Alexandrov and Ivan Mikhailov). They were all defeated.[9] It was the same picture in the USSR, whether with Makhno and his Ukrainian anarchists, with the counter-revolutionary Ungarn-Sternberg in Mongolia or with the 'Basmachis' in the emirate of Bukhara[10] who fought from 1918 to about 1928. Nor was the 1936-39 Palestinian guerrilla movement against the Jewish settlers in British-mandated Palestine victorious either. In short, guerrilla tactics in the Afro-Asian colonial countries scored no clear successes before the Second World War.

Latin America was a very different context; for a start, there was no foreign interference. After civil wars which had seen a mixture of regular and irregular operations, the insurgents were successful in Mexico, and (after six years of fighting from 1927 to 1933) the populist leader Sandino was victorious in Nicaragua.

In China, the remnants of the Red Army,[11] whose survival was due to their withdrawing some 10,000 km, managed to establish a sanctuary in Yenan province in 1935 and consolidate their position there. The Japanese aggression began two years later; Mao Zedong had just completed the first of his three basic works on revolutionary war.[12]

In order to wage a modern war, the dominated elites must first assimilate the conceptual tools of modernity, above all the ideology of nationalism. This is not as simple as it might appear; in fact, the spread of nationalism over the last fifty years has been far from automatic. The elites must also know their adversary: rarely has the slogan 'learn from the enemy' had more meaning than for colonized peoples. As for the type of organization, it has usually been the mass party or the vanguard party, based originally on European models.

Patriotic resistance movements are generally characterized by their spontaneity. First they erupt and then they are organized. Revolutionary guerrilla warfare, on the other hand, is planned and organized from the top and spreads gradually as it finds support. The traditional guerrilla movements did not have permanent fighting forces.[13] (Shaka's Zulu armies were an exception.) Fighting broke out more or less spontaneously (and never occurred at harvest-time) and was under the leadership of traditional chiefs. People were resisting the destruction of an order they sought to restore. Outside the field of military tactics or weaponry, innovations were unknown.

Whereas a patriotic resistance movement aims to drive out the invaders and restore the previous legitimacy, a revolutionary guerrilla movement wants to seize power and establish a new order.

In the initial stages, a revolutionary guerrilla movement can use rudimentary weapons; but its conceptual tools and strategic vision must be developed politically, militarily and, above all, organizationally. As it progresses, such a movement absorbs, to adopt Amilcar Cabral's expression, 'what the world has conquered in the service of humanity'.[14]

Modern guerrilla movements belong within a specific historical framework: the Second World War, the rise of Asian and then African nationalism, the gradual ending of colonialism and the disappearance of the imperial outlook in Europe, given the new spirit of the times.

What is known as revolutionary war originates from Mao Zedong. Though not apparent from his writings, Mao's political innovation consisted in using the Leninist vanguard party to mobilize and lead the peasantry. This is unorthodox because the vanguard party claims to mobilize and lead the urban proletariat. In strictly military terms, Mao's original contribution lay in using both regular and irregular units within the framework of irregular operations — these were intended to lead to a conventional confrontation once they had built up sufficient strength. Added to these innovations, in which the political and the military were closely intertwined, was the nationalist phenomenon: the Japanese invasion of 1937-45 led to an acceptance of the leadership role of the Communist Party, the incarnation of Chinese nationalism.

Mao's military thought met with opposition, both before and after the Long March. But he resisted those within the movement who wanted to form a regular army straight away:

> In general, we should not struggle at all costs against 'the guerrilla spirit', but recognize honestly that the Red Army has the character of an army of guerrillas. There is nothing to be ashamed about. On the contrary, the guerrilla character constitutes our peculiarity, our strong side, the instrument of our victory over the enemy. We must prepare ourselves one day to give up the character of an army of guerrillas that our army has, but, for the present, that is impossible. [He added:] [We are] *against* the purely military viewpoint and the idea of roving insurgents, but *for* the view that the Red Army is a propagandist and organizer of the Chinese revolution.[15]

Consequently, Mao advocated: mobile warfare with small rear areas (no adventurism during offensive operations; no seeking to retain territory at any cost while on the defensive); a command that was not highly centralized, so as to leave the guerrilla corps with the necessary flexibility; and a Red Army that was constantly propagandizing and organizing.

The rest of Mao's military strategy was conventional. He stressed the importance of intelligence, which allows the guerrillas to select the most advantageous time and place for an attack, and of familiarity with local conditions, which ensures initial military superiority in a particular area. He spoke of the need both to harass the enemy while keeping the initiative, and to create the conditions for victory even before the battle has begun by demoralizing the adversary.

Mao's originality lies in his political contribution and in his linking the political and the military. The Japanese occupation cemented the alliance between the Communist Party and the peasantry. The behaviour of the Japanese troops, the terror and devastation they caused, and the harshness of their occupation (the Nazis made a similar error in the Ukraine), forced the peasants to react. The traditional rural elites fled the Japanese-occupied zones and those who collaborated with the Japanese were never subsequently accepted as legitimate rulers. The way was clear for the Red Army, which organized a sustained campaign of anti-Japanese propaganda. By designating the Communists as their principal enemies, the Japanese themselves had enhanced the Communists' prestige.

The Chinese Communists had a three-pronged military structure: the Red Army, regional guerrilla groups of full-time partisans, and local militias. This structure was to be imitated all over the world, from Vietnam to the Portuguese colonies. Each unit of the army had its political commissar, whose duties included relations with the local population. An army that did not molest the peasants, and declared itself — in its deeds — to be at the service of the people, was a new concept in traditional societies. The army's numerous political and administrative tasks were allocated to various departments: organization; propaganda and education; co-operation with civilians; work on the enemy. In the war zones proper, the organized population built roads, acted as guides and provided food and information. In the guerrilla-held zones, the population helped organize the resistance, liquidated traitors and, when necessary, destroyed communications.

When the Red Army surrounded a village, it first explained why it was fighting and then promulgated a series of measures: a reduction in taxes (by about a quarter); distribution of food to the poor; organization of the young into self-defence militias; creation of mass movements to resist the Japanese. A propaganda unit, usually made up of cadres who were from the next region to be invested, was detailed to open up a new guerrilla front.

The cadres had to have in-depth knowledge of local problems such as economic conditions and the specific nature of any grievances. This required detailed preparation. The cadres obviously had to speak the regional languages or dialects. They infiltrated, dressed as peasants and were charged with making the initial contact with the population. Their task was to find those villagers prepared to support the anti-Japanese resistance. At the regional level, support was sought not only from the peasantry but also from other social strata: artisans, students, secondary-school pupils, and so on. Even bandits had their uses: they were sent into the combat zones (though never into the red bases). In time, assemblies were set up with elected representatives. Though their political power was limited, it was through them that the masses felt psychologically integrated into the resistance.

The eight years of anti-Japanese struggle firmly established the Communists in their bastion in the north. But in 1945 no one saw them as winners. The USSR was negotiating with the Nationalist government and, in exchange for Outer Mongolia, recognized the legitimacy of Chiang Kai-shek. When the Chinese Communists were finally victorious, it was due to their own efforts and despite their relative numerical inferiority. The reasons for their success date not from the years 1945-49, however, but from the previous period.

The Chinese model has only really been imitated by the Vietnamese, who have added their own variations and particular slant. But its broad concepts and organizational techniques have been taken up by numerous movements, including non-Marxist-Leninist ones.

The term guerrilla movement covers very diverse realities. A typology can be drawn up, according to ideological motivation: (1) liberation movements struggling against a colonial power or foreign occupier; (2) revolutionary movements in independent countries and based on social (or religious) demands; and (3) minority ethnic and/or religious movements demanding secession or autonomy.

There are many different ideologies, though nationalism has been by far the most important in modern times. They can usually be divided into the following broad categories: (1) Marxist-Leninist; (2) nationalist without any reference to class struggle; (3) conservative, seeking to maintain or restore a social or political order in opposition to an established regime of a different type; and (4) reactionary (in the etymological sense of the word), aiming for a return to a real or imagined past.

Guerrilla movements spring up for many reasons. They may be a response to ethnic or religious oppression that, at a particular moment in time, comes to be perceived as unacceptable. They may result from social discontent that has reached breaking-point, often triggered off by something quite minor. For the last four decades, however, the catalyst has usually been a small voluntaristic movement whose aim is to win over the population by enlightening it.

The vanguard group is often very small at first. The Chinese Communist Party had twelve members when it was founded in 1921; the African Party for the Independence of Guinea and Cape Verde (PAIGC) had six founding members in 1956. The leading group's first aim is to understand its own society. It must identify the sociological imbalance, work out an appropriate strategy in the current conditions, identify the social sectors that are sensitized and easily mobilized, and assess the adversary's political and military weaknesses, on both the domestic and the international level.

We know in fact that the unfolding behaviour (development) of a phenomenon-in-motion, whatever its external conditioning, depends mainly on its internal characteristics. We also know that on the political level — however fine and attractive the reality of others may be — we can only truly transform our own reality on the basis of detailed knowledge of it and our own efforts and sacrifices.

It is worth recalling in this Tricontinental gathering, so rich in experience and examples, that however great the similarity between our cases and however identical our enemies, unfortunately or fortunately national liberation and social revolution are not exportable commodities. They are (and increasingly so every day) a local, national product — more or less influenced by (favourable and unfavourable) external factors, but essentially determined and conditioned by the historical reality of each people.[16]

At this stage, the first members are recruited to form the core of the party. They are made aware of oppression and its nature, and of the vulnerability of the oppressors. The most easily mobilized elements are often the young city-dwellers; semi-intellectual or semi-educated, *déclassé* or marginalized, they have no prospects and are seething with latent discontent. It is far more difficult to mobilize the most disinherited, those who have no hope of change, and whose long habits of subservience and absolute poverty have given them little taste for risk-taking. It is vital to train middle-ranking cadres. The higher cadres generally exist already; they are in the leadership or among the intellectuals who soon come over to the movement. The middle-ranking cadres will do the essential political work on the ground: propaganda, explanation, cadre-formation, organization. Step by step, this minority will provide the masses with both the motivation to act against the established order and the organizational know-how.

The next stage consists in winning over 'mass support', that is, the support of a part of the population (rarely exceeding a quarter of it). Persuasion, indoctrination, the selective use of terror to eliminate enemy agents, intimidation and agitation — all these tactics are used. The difficult, delicate mobilization process must lead, on the one hand, to the establishment of an underground political infrastructure among the population and, on the other, to the wide dissemination of the movement's programme and slogans.

In the Leninist model, organizational strategy consists in forming a mass base out of a small group of disciplined militants. This strategy presupposes that the state is unpopular, as was increasingly the case in the colonial context following the Second World War. It would be much more difficult to mobilize the masses in an independent country on social bases or around minority issues since nationalism is no longer an issue.

The Maoist and Vietnamese variant (developed during the first and second Vietnam wars), which spread through the colonial and semi-colonial world, lays even greater emphasis on massive popular support, the peasantry, and the protracted nature of the armed struggle.

The support — and control — of the population offsets the advantages enjoyed by the state, i.e. government control over the administration, the police and the army.

During this stage — which sees intense propaganda and agitation — attempts are made to recruit leaders or local figures who might be able to bring over a section of the population. Attempts are also made to infiltrate institutions and to foment strikes or demonstrations, if circumstances allow. Here the best policy is to stir up movements only if they are certain to succeed, for the psychological effect of failure often results in the loss of months of patient work which could otherwise have been effective and borne fruit.

A guerrilla movement can survive only with the support of that part of the population on which it depends for information, communications, food and recruits. This support is a function of the underground political organization. Broader support, when it comes, merely demonstrates the erosion of the state's authority.

Selective terrorism — in both the countryside and the

towns — may be directed against agents of the state and those collaborating with them, or against the adversary's forces, whether armed or not. In both cases, the purpose is not to win a military victory, but to weaken the state's control and will. In a colonial situation, the combination of guerrilla warfare and selective terrorism aims, in the long run, to bring about negotiations.

While the underground political infrastructure is of fundamental importance and must be cherished, the passive support of the population should not be underestimated. The population must identify with the overall objectives and programme of those fighting. At certain times, an act of refusal by the masses may be decisive. In reality, the revolutionary guerrilla movement's political objective is the population itself. The movement's propaganda aims to demoralize those who support the adversary passively, and to persuade or indoctrinate those who are neutral.

To gain the support of the population, the insurgents seek to show, first, that the adversary, though usually seen as unbeatable, is in fact vulnerable, and, second, that the struggle is just. This is done through selective terrorism, making spectacular attacks on the enemy or carrying out acts of sabotage that demonstrate the revolutionary organization's effectiveness.

When the leader is perceived as charismatic, the population is quicker to come over. The ideological force of the cause for which he is fighting, whether nationalism, liberty or social justice, is the revolutionary organization's main strength. Marxism–Leninism, which seems to offer a coherent explanation of the world and its conflicts, continues to provide a mobilizing ideology. When the enemy is defined as imperialism and its associated local strata, this results in a clear, credible target. But whatever the social goals, nationalism is the fundamental ideological motivation behind movements struggling against foreign domination.

One of the functions of ideology is to identify friends and

enemies clearly. Revealing the workings of the corrupt system and its inability to respond to the needs and aspirations of the masses — particularly of the intelligentsia, a painfully conscious stratum — acts as a highly mobilizing factor.

The liberation movement aims to foment disorder, gum up the administrative machine and disrupt the economy, in short, to undermine the authority of the state. Disorder is easy to create, but costly and difficult to deal with. The army and the police have to keep a constant watch on every possible target whereas one or two operations by the guerrilla group are enough to have the desired effect. In military terms, guerrilla warfare develops gradually; its initial impact is usually psychological.

In the beginning, when the guerrillas have the initiative, the element of surprise should in principle allow easy successes that raise the combatants' morale and show public opinion or the peasants that the movement is active and effective. What counts most, not merely on the military level but more generally, is the guerrillas' training. Its aim is to instil a solid ideological motivation, backed up by discipline.

What is the social origin of those who take part in popular insurgencies in the Third World in general? It is often the 'semi-educated' who join the middle-ranking cadres and the peasants who join the troops. The role of the party (a cadre is priest, teacher and helper all rolled into one) is to inculcate in all these elements a devotion to the cause, a sense of responsibility and group solidarity, a new (modern) notion of time that is essential for military operations, a respect for equipment and a concern for efficiency. This patient training goes against the grain in most, if not all, traditional societies.

In practice, the revolutionaries' ideal of the 'new man' is represented by the fighter, not by the peace-time builder of the economy. Who would have bet on Mao Zedong winning in 1945? Who in 1946 could have imagined that the Viet Minh would end up winning a battle of the importance of Dien Bien Phu?

Guerrilla Warfare

The revolutionary guerrilla movement is a permanent school: for the middle-ranking cadres, for men and women at the base, for the population. Every movement can instantly be identified by the style of its militants. Vietnamese and Eritreans (of the EPLF) have much in common, whereas Palestinians from Fatah, and more particularly the Afghan resistance in general, are at the opposite end of the spectrum.

The hard, prolonged struggle means that the party must be strong, disciplined and austere — in a word, militarized. The Marxist-Leninist-type party is a remarkable war machine, with its clandestinity, organization and degree of control. It is capable of sustaining the long struggle in its darkest hours, yet once victory has been won it becomes a primarily bureaucratic and police instrument rather than a force promoting social and economic development.

During the struggle, the party endeavours to create a common front with its allies. But its role is to be the leader. Given its organization, cohesion, discipline, doctrinal austerity and harsh methods of internal control, it remains (provided it has capitalized on nationalism) superior to the other groups and organizations, which are mere satellites. Once the party has taken power, it will move inexorably to marginalize and then eliminate other organizations. This so-called transition stage does not usually last long.

The 'time dimension' is of vital importance during the struggle, since it allows the party to gather strength and, ultimately, to win a military as well as a political victory. With time as the decisive factor, the state machine must be overthrown. The revolutionary guerrilla movement is fighting a political power based on an administration, a police force and an army. If the insurgency manages to control the population and gain its support, both active and passive, it can triumph. The battle for control of the population is the essential characteristic of revolutionary guerrilla warfare, which is above all a political war. Wherever the guerrilla movement has military control over an area (or where it has a clandestine presence in regions controlled by the adversary) it endeavours to create what have aptly been called 'parallel hierarchies'.[17]

This means organizing elections to appoint a new administration (such as the village assembly), which then has the task of running the village in accordance with the revolutionary movement's political and military objectives and creating a self-defence militia among the young. If the party controls the region, it must try to set up a dispensary and a school in each village (or group of villages). In short, it must take the place of the state. The movement's legitimacy will be shown by the good behaviour of its militants, by its contribution to the welfare of the population and by its strength. The combatants' attitude towards the local population is of vital importance. It is what distinguishes the movement from the army, whether it be colonial and hence foreign, or local and almost by definition arrogant, corrupt and predatory. The guerrilla movement's behaviour towards the population is its 'visiting card'.

In liberated regions, the movement relies on the fraction of the population that actively supports the struggle. The links with this fraction must be permanent and cannot be taken for granted. Support may be lost through psychological error, injustice or weariness. Constant explaining, indoctrination and persuasion are needed. Force must be used only as a last resort. The population's desire for security can be manipulated by the army. This must never be forgotten, either in the initial stages of the struggle when the guerrilla movement has only tenuous links with the population, or later on when the war becomes protracted and aggravates difficulties in the rural areas.

If the guerrilla movement eventually succeeds in controlling a 'liberated region', it becomes the guarantor of law and order. It tries to show the gulf between the corruption, oppression and inefficiency of the state and the movement's own justice, good behaviour and achievements.[18]

On the military level, since the guerrilla movement is not confined to one region, it tries to ensure that the opposing armed forces are spread out thinly over as wide an area as possible. By waging the struggle in both the countryside and the towns (using sabotage and selective terrorism), the movement forces the adversary to mobilize large numbers of his forces in an unfavourable psychological climate.

At the start of operations, the guerrilla movement always has the initiative and must make the most of an advantage that will later be contested. The choice of terrain is important for the initial implantation.[19] The movement's terrain is basically the population itself. This explains how an armed guerrilla movement could be set up in flat country like the Yugoslav Voivodina or the Red River delta in Vietnam. It would be absurd, however, to ignore the vital importance of the physical nature of the terrain. Mountains, jungles, forests, marshlands and boscage can all become places of refuge. As long as the movement is mobile and knows how to use the terrain, even the desert can be favourable — as the Polisario Front has shown.

A country's size is also relevant. In a small territory like Guinea-Bissau (36,125 sq km), it was relatively easy to organize a sizeable guerrilla movement like Amilcar Cabral's. Conversely, in a very large country, particularly one that is sparsely inhabited, a movement may find itself marking time without ever managing to dominate the terrain. In principle, however, a large country with a reasonable level of population is an advantage for a guerrilla movement if it manages not to confine itself to one local area. Small zones are usually easy to control by government forces, unless the terrain is exceptionally favourable to the guerrilla movement. For liberation movements struggling against foreign domination, a sizeable population (especially a large rural population) is a decided advantage. In the towns, however, control and repression are easier.

Let us now move from the general to the particular. Apart

from securing the support of the population, the most important thing is to set up bases where the guerrillas can be relatively safe. These bases are vital if the movement has no sanctuary in a neighbouring country.

Bad weather conditions (the rainy season or winter) are not necessarily a disadvantage for the guerrillas. The monsoon rains may prove a logistical handicap, for example, yet they also make flying difficult. Ultimately, both terrain and climate are factors that the most skilful and determined movements use to their advantage. Subjective factors such as the determination to win are, however, probably more important for both sides. Contrary to what the victor may say in retrospect, the outcome is very rarely a foregone conclusion. Given determination and adaptability, the state is rarely — at least in the initial stages — at a disadvantage. The denser the communications network, the less safe the guerrilla movement is — counter-insurgencies build roads. A poor communications network, as in Afghanistan, is a considerable advantage for the insurgents.

Nevertheless, the decisive military factor is the quality of the state's response. At first, the problem of weapons is relatively unimportant for the guerrilla movement. Its needs are limited, given the small number of members: it is enough to have a few guns or machine-guns and small quantities of grenades or mines. The element of surprise in the initial operations should, in principle, make it possible to pick up weapons. This is always easy at the beginning of an insurgency — and at the end, when the victorious guerrilla force seizes towns and villages. Once the guerrilla movement has succeeded in establishing a foothold, political commissars and fighters can be sent out to regions or zones seen as sympathetic. In the initial stage, it is sensible to increase the likelihood of success by operating far from enemy centres, in areas where communications are poor. The fighters need time to become war-hardened. Since they have the initiative and can play on the element of surprise, some easy successes will boost their confidence. The first operations are not usually followed by an immediate pursuit and the guerrillas have time to withdraw in good order.

Selective terrorism, which plays only a minor role in a rural guerrilla war of any size, has several functions: not only, as already mentioned, to eliminate enemy agents or carry out sabotage operations, but to gain recognition through the impact on the media (in the towns). In the countryside, selective terrorism makes it possible to loosen the enemy's administrative grip, and to win over the population if the state and its agents are unpopular.

Violence is a delicate instrument. It may act as a catalyst, but it can also act as a deterrent; it can even be totally counter-productive. This applies both to the guerrilla movement and to the state. Excessive repression provokes a profound resentment that mobilizes the people. In countries where different communities co-exist, indiscriminate terror — a particularly cruel form of terrorism — sometimes aims to create divisions between ethnic groups. This was the strategy of the Algerian National Liberation Front (FLN) in the towns in 1957, where bombs were placed in public places frequented by Europeans. It should be pointed out that the weaker the guerrilla movement is, the stronger the temptation to turn to urban terrorism.

When the state is foreign and its repression progressively fails to discriminate between the innocent and the guilty, violence becomes counter-productive — unless it turns into organized, systematic and wide-scale massacres. A good example is the Guatemalan state's treatment of its Indian majority from 1981 to 1982.

From start to finish, it is organization that allows the guerrilla movement to survive in face of the enemy's crushing material superiority. The more extensive the movement's organization, the less vulnerable it is. It is important for it not to remain a regional movement. From 1960 to the Sandinistas' victory in 1979, *localismo* was a typical failing of most, if not all, the Latin American guerrilla forces. With its lack of military strength, the guerrilla movement needs to be particularly well organized. It must have an integrated strategy and slogans that are efficently relayed from the centre to the combatants. This cohesion is the result of tough fights at the top; the political leadership has no choice but to demonstrate the greatest firmness when in command. The existence of an undisputed leader who commands respect will make organizational discipline easier. War is not a suitable arena for democratic debate.

The guerrilla movement seeks to create a threefold military structure: first, a mobile and well-armed liberation army that uses partisan tactics, but is able, when circumstances allow, to transform itself into a conventional army (China and the Viet Minh); second, regional guerrilla forces to harass the enemy locally, provide intelligence and logistics, and so on (the most competent elements among the regional forces can be recruited into the liberation army); and finally, local militias whose importance lies in psychological and political mobilization rather than in strictly military terms (the best elements can be transferred to the regional forces). Apart from the local militias, all the armed forces are full-time guerrillas. The correct strategy is always to keep the initiative and to avoid all frontal assaults, unless the threatened base is seen as vital (as was the case with the EPLF between 1979 and 1984 in the Sahel, where six Ethiopian offensives were halted by hard-fought trench defences). The guerrilla movement must paralyse the enemy while picking away at his positions through the establishment of new parallel hierarchies.

This description may give the impression of continuous fighting, of a never-ending trial of strength. Apart from certain critical moments, however, the situation on the ground is often a stalemate. In some guerrilla wars, weeks go by with nothing happening. Once a certain equilibrium has been reached, it is tempting, for both the guerrillas and the army, to hold on as best they can, without taking further risks. So deeply rooted is the desire for security that it wins out at the least opportunity. It is up to the leadership to watch over the activities of the troops.

The guerrillas soon have to set up arsenals, field hospitals, workshops to repair weapons, and so on. The less dependence on the outer world, the better. But problems of logistics soon become crucial.

It is extremely rare for a victorious guerrilla movement not to have outside support, and most have had sanctuaries. (The only two exceptions are China and Cuba.) The Yugoslavs had their arms and equipment parachuted in during the war. China alone, thanks to its enormous size, the existence of solid bases and the final collapse of the Japanese forces, was able to do without sanctuaries and outside supplies. As for Cuba, the shortest guerrilla war among the victorious struggles of the last forty years (lasting less than thirty months), it could do without material help: it never had to arm more than some 500 men, and faced a state with no mass base and lacking the necessary determination.

Material support becomes vital when the guerrilla movement has grown in size and can no longer capture sufficient supplies from the enemy. The attitude of a neighbouring state or states is then critical. Any neighbouring state that gives material support is running a grave risk if the guerrilla movement's adversary is determined to strike, whether directly or indirectly. South Africa put such pressure (direct and indirect) on Mozambique between 1981 and 1983 that the latter was forced to end its aid to the African National Congress (ANC) in its fight against apartheid.

While material aid (such as arms and medical supplies) is obviously necessary, it should not obscure the importance of political and moral support at the international level. Public opinion, especially (if it can be reached) among the adversary, and indirect political help from international bodies both have a role to play.

In terms of external aid, however, the existence of a sanctuary is undoubtedly the decisive factor. Without an Algerian sanctuary, where would Polisario be? Without a sanctuary in Pakistan, how long could the Afghan resistance hold out? A sanctuary almost always provides a breathing space for the guerrilla movement. Everything must be done to protect it and ensure access to it. If the supply lines are cut, the end of the guerrilla movement is not far off (as in the case of the Dhofar resistance in 1976).

It is equally important for the guerrilla movement to have access to a minimum of surgical facilities, both inside and outside the country.[20] It is vital for the fighters' morale to know they will receive medical attention.

Nevertheless, every seriously organized guerrilla movement is well advised to rely mainly on its own resources. If outside help is too easily obtained (as in the case of the Palestinians), it encourages neither self-reliance nor the virtues of self-denial. In a war, the most important qualities, apart from strategic intelligence and an imaginative leadership, are determination, tenacity and a devotion to the cause. Nothing else can explain the EPLF's ability to hold out over the long years of withdrawal, from 1979 to 1984. Too much aid may even lead to failure, as in the case of Mustafa Barzani in Iraqi Kurdistan in 1975. (The Shah of Iran had not only halted all supplies of heavy weapons to the movement — a fatal change in policy, since the Kurds were engaged in conventional warfare. He had also closed the sanctuary in order to negotiate advantageous terms with Iraq.)

The second stage, the one that follows political implantation and the beginnings of military operations, is generally very long. Military operations are now expanded and — particularly important — 'parallel hierarchies' are set up. During this phase, it is vital for the movement to show clemency to prisoners. There is no better encouragement to fight than the knowledge that the adversary gives no quarter.

Once a certain equilibrium has been reached, the revolutionary guerrilla movement must decide where to deliver the decisive blow (or blows) that will break the adversary's will to fight. The strength — and hence the morale — of the regular army now declines while that of the revolutionaries increases.

Very few revolutionary guerrilla movements have reached the stage of mobile warfare with a full-scale battle which is a prelude to the final campaign of annihilation. Mao and Giap remain the exceptions. The only other (minor) instances can be counted on the fingers of one hand: Cuba, Cambodia, Nicaragua.

It should be stressed that virtually the only example of a national liberation movement's winning a purely military victory against an industrial power is Dien Bien Phu. In an international (and domestic) climate that is increasingly anti-war, violence has almost without exception forced the metropole to negotiate. These negotiations have always been the outcome of a long war effort by the liberation movement: they result from the psychological and political crisis transplanted into the metropole itself. Negotiations have also come about because the metropole did not think the game was worth the candle. In Vietnam the US could not win a victory on the ground, given its self-imposed restrictions (no escalation, and so on), but the Vietnam war was also lost in the United States itself. After the psychological shock of the Tet offensive in 1968, the peace movement kept up a constant barrage of opposition. This had an undeniable impact. The war was perceived as morally unjust, the state's declared objective as unconvincing. The war was not only costly in men and money, it was also unpopular because the US was failing to win it. Despite propaganda about the danger of Communist expansion throughout South-East Asia, neither public opinion nor Congress itself was convinced that vital US security interests were at stake. Conversely, the outcome of the war was vital for both North Vietnam and the National Liberation Front (NLF). The

United States should have made certain it was capable of estimating the Saigon regime's ability to win a sufficient social base as well as judging the strength of its will to survive. The Korean war proved to be a misleading precedent in American political and strategic calculations.

It cannot be taken for granted that a guerrilla movement will win against a colonial power, however. The British defeated the (Chinese) Communist insurgents in Malaya (1948-57) by resettling the population and above all by promising independence — once the guerrilla movement had been crushed — to the traditional ruling (Muslim) Malay strata. In Kenya, the Mau Mau movement (one of the few movements without a modernist leadership[21] in the last forty years) was also crushed (1952-56).

Revolutionary guerrilla movements in independent countries pose altogether different problems. Here no negotiations are possible and victory must be won militarily. Otherwise the movement is either wiped out or forced to try to survive as long as possible in very difficult conditions.

In the Philippines (1948-50),[22] the Huks were defeated by a combination of three factors: independence had just been granted; the movement had always remained regionalized; and the state took decisive, effective military and political action.

In independent countries, there are two vital factors: first and foremost, the strength of the state — by strength is meant not brutal repression by specially trained troops, but above all the determination of the state to maintain its authority — and, second, the depth of its social base.

In Nicaragua the Somoza regime's brutal repression was legendary. The regime's corruption and negligence, combined with its anachronistic despotism, had gradually left it with no more than a tiny social base and its own praetorian guard.

There are very few examples of successful revolutionary guerrilla wars in independent countries. The Communist insurgency in Greece from 1947 to 1949 was defeated: it enjoyed only limited popular support, its strategy of frontal assaults was wrong and its logistic resources were destroyed after the Tito-Stalin break in 1948, while the government forces' performance, backed by the British and Americans, improved considerably.

As already mentioned, the Cuban guerrilla movement has the peculiar distinction of having fought the shortest guerrilla war in the history of insurgency movements over the last forty years. The Cuban model of the *foco*[23] will not be discussed here. Its many failures in Latin America during the 1960s are well known and have led to self-criticism by some of its strongest advocates. Suffice it to say that the Cuban victory is to be explained less by the alleged strategic innovation of the *foco* than by three essential factors. The first of these was the support of a large part of the urban population for the anti-Batista struggle, given that there was initially no question of a Marxist-Leninist-type revolution. In the beginning, Castroism fought the Batista tyranny for 'bread and liberty' in the name of a 'humanist revolution' with populist undertones. The second factor was the Batista regime's social isolation and its lack of determination to combat the insurgency: the state simply collapsed. Finally, there was the benevolent neutrality of the United States.

Over the last quarter of a century, Latin America has seen only two victories of armed insurgencies — in Cuba and Nicaragua. In Africa, on the other hand, no independent regime has yet been overthrown as a result of a protracted armed struggle. The armed movements in southern Sudan forced Khartoum to concede autonomy in the 1970s, but it is not certain today that the region will preserve its special status. Eritrea is marking time despite an outstanding struggle (it was on the point of victory in 1978 before the Soviets supplied Ethiopia with the material means for a counteroffensive).

In the Middle East, the two Kurdish insurgencies — in Iraq (1961-75) and Iran (since 1979) — have been unable to win despite considerable popular support. These are, again, instances of minority struggles in independent (and non-democratic) countries. Within the framework of the United Nations, the only struggles to have received significant support are those directed against Western states. Internal struggles in African and Asian countries, on the other hand, have found virtually no support. Thus the right to self-determination is limited to the right of colonized peoples to liberate themselves (except in the special cases of Eritrea and the Western Sahara).

The Marxist-Leninist guerrilla movement in Dhofar (southern Arabia), though remarkably well organized, was quietly put down in 1976 by a combination of British 'advisers', the forces of the Sultan of Oman and an Iranian expeditionary corps (plus some Jordanian units) which were able to cut the guerrillas' supply lines from South Yemen.

Generally speaking, minority struggles are crushed with the blessing of states. They exist in almost total isolation — unless inter-state rivalries lead one state to want to weaken another by aiding the rebels. In the case of the Kurds, this type of ethno-strategy, notably between Iran and Iraq, has been practised for over two decades. Neither country wants to see the insurgents win; it is simply a question of weakening the rival state. Thus in 1983 Iraq, which was supplying arms to the Iranian Kurds, allowed Turkish troops to 'clean up' its own frontier regions held by the Kurds, regions it was no longer able to control effectively.

If East Pakistan was able to become Bangladesh, it owes it above all to Indian troops, Indira Gandhi being only too happy to deliver a sharp blow to the rival state of Pakistan.

The complex phenomenon of guerrilla movements does not lend itself to generalizations. There are, however, certain general laws, in addition to conditions that largely determine a movement's failure or success.

The case of the Afghan resistance is interesting in this respect. It began at the end of 1978 with a series of spontaneous regional uprisings which had their origins in the rejection of government decisions affecting general policy as well as religious, social, ethnic and other questions, and which were initially directed against a Marxist-Leninist regime. This regime lacked social bases in the countryside and its support was limited to Kabul. In 1979, the uprising spread throughout Afghanistan. After the Soviet intervention (Christmas 1979), another dimension was added to the mere rejection of the Kabul regime: the struggle against the foreigner. More than half a dozen movements, three 'fundamentalist' and three 'traditionalist', fought for what were often regional audiences. They were marked by the lack of an overall strategy, limited tactical skill and massive but unorganized support. With the exception of the Panjshir Valley (led by an extremely able political and military strategist) and a few local leaders applying the organizational methods of the Panjshir (inspired by revolutionary guerrilla movements), almost all limited to the north-east of the country, the guerrilla war was fought along traditional lines.

Thanks to the Pakistani sanctuary which allowed the movement of arms, munitions, doctors and medicines, and despite a growing number of refugees (about 3 million), the Afghan resistance has grown considerably over the last five years. In the face of such unexpected, wide-scale resistance, the Soviets opted for a long-term strategy. This involved three principal elements. First, the number of armed forces deployed was initially limited to 100,000 men, and then perhaps to some 120,000, which were to hold Kabul at first and then take other towns and main roads. Second came a growing dependence of the Afghan economy on the Soviet Union and a patient attempt to establish the regime firmly — though difficult to measure, this does not seem to have borne fruit. The third and most important factor was the lack of any really effective counter-insurgency, at least from

1980 to 1984 (apart from a few devastating lightning strikes in 1984). The lightning strikes were carried out by tanks, the air force and the artillery; little use was made of airborne troops; and there was no systematic pursuit designed to cut off the adversary's lines of communication.

With the exception of the paratroops, the Soviet army (an army of conscripts) is ponderous and not very effective — despite its fire-power — in a war of this type. However, since armies also exist in order to fight — a truth that is sometimes forgotten in these pacifist times in the West — Afghanistan provides an excellent testing-ground for an army that has done no fighting since the Second World War. It is worth noting that this is not the case of the French, American and British armies, whose troops have fought in numerous theatres over the last forty years.

If the Afghan resistance is to survive, it must retain its control over the mountain areas, use permanent troops rather than traditional guerrillas, and build up a solid logistical capability — this means having transport, engineers and communications, in addition to effective anti-aircraft weapons. Meanwhile the fighters hope that the Pakistani sanctuary will remain open to them. But they can count neither on a Soviet troop withdrawal (due to lack of pressure from public opinion in the USSR), nor on a Soviet military defeat. This war of attrition is devastating for the populace and its duration depends largely on the haven in Pakistan; yet in the long run, the Afghans cannot win. For the Soviets, there can be no question of withdrawing from Afghanistan on a note of failure. Withdrawal is conceivable only if the Kabul regime can ensure its own survival.

The last vestige of guerrilla warfare is its use by South Africa in Angola and Mozambique, and later by the United States on the borders of Nicaragua, to destabilize 'Marxist-Leninist' regimes that are themselves the product of an armed insurgency. The characteristic feature of these guerrilla wars, notably in Mozambique and Nicaragua (the case of Angola is more complex),[24] is that they have no need of popular support. A sanctuary, commando operations based on sabotage, and harassment are sufficient if carried out on a large enough scale to force the state into an exhausting permanent mobilization. This leads to economic paralysis and general upheaval. The signing of the 1984 Nkomati Accord between Mozambique and South Africa, which has deprived the ANC of a sanctuary, is thus very important for South Africa and a major blow to any future development of the armed struggle. But here we are already in the area of counter-insurgency.

3
Counter-Insurgency

Counter-insurgency, as its name suggests, is a response to insurgency; it is one of its consequences. In this sense, the initiative does not lie with the counter-insurgency, at least over a given period — its whole strategy consists in seizing the initiative from the enemy:

> Any sensible government should attempt to defeat an insurgent movement during the subversive build-up phase before it enters the guerrilla phase, and if that is not possible owing to circumstances perhaps outside the government's control, then the movement must be defeated as early as possible during the guerrilla phase. Unfortunately, during the build-up phase, the signs are not always recognized, and the existence of a subversive movement may even be ignored or denied for short-sighted political reasons.[1]

What cause is counter-insurgency fighting against? The first thing is to understand the adversary, the nature of the struggle and the strategy of the insurgency. These questions may seem obvious, yet they deserve thinking about. Chiang Kai-shek's major failing was his inability to grasp the nature of the challenge posed by the Chinese Communists. At least he had the excuse of it being a historical 'first'. Subsequently, however, in the first Indochina war, the French General Staff again underestimated the adversary. The lessons of the war were only drawn afterwards. Applying these lessons to Algeria produced military results. But there was a political contradiction here — what was actually needed was to do what the British had done in Malaya, in other words, to offer independence and not the status of a French *département*, something that was no longer in tune with the spirit of the times. The war would have had meaning only if the FLN had been Marxist-Leninist and France had conceded independence to some nationalist force.[2] In practice, the Portuguese army only began to understand the situation in the 'overseas provinces' several years after the struggle had begun: Spinola in Angola in 1966-67, and then in Guinea-Bissau from 1968 onwards. (Conversely, it is the Palestinian organizations that have been slow to understand why Israel cannot be defeated.)

Naturally enough, people today think they know the whys and wherefores of guerrilla warfare. Yet each situation is unique. It is not enough to apply a particular military strategy and hope that it will resolve a problem all too easily labelled an 'insurgency'.

Although the initiative does not lie with the state, it has a number of advantages in the beginning: army, police, administration, foreign aid, financial resources, control of information. Above all, it almost always benefits from the passivity of the majority of the population.

Once the nature of the insurgency has been determined and its structures and methods are known, the state is fighting against political subversion at least as much as against the armed insurgents.

To mount an adequate counter-insurgency operation calls for a co-ordinated political, military, police and administrative strategy. There are two vital factors: on the one hand, determination, resolute action and skilful handling by the state and, on the other, the existence of even a few social bases.

It is not true to say that the state needs the support of the population to win. So long as the guerrilla movement lacks the support of, and fails to control, a large part of the population (which is rare) the state needs only a relatively limited social base. Yet it is generally to the state's advantage to introduce concrete improvements, even if they are limited (dispensaries, schools, food programmes, etc.), for the deprived sectors it seeks to win over.

The most pressing tasks lie elsewhere, however. On the one hand, political subversion must be kept to a minimum. Here intelligence has a vital role to play. The state will try to seize the initiative from the insurgents by harassing them with its mobile forces, and by forcing them to expend their energy on defence and mere survival. The state will attack the guerrilla forces in zones where they are implanted, hunt them down and use commando squads to lay night ambushes. Above all, it will (after a long reconnaissance period) threaten and destroy the guerrillas' logistic resources, such as lines of communication and food supplies.

Anti-guerrilla offensives can only be mounted by mobile, well-motivated specialist troops led by competent and respected officers. In an underdeveloped country this amounts to a contradiction in terms: for officers in many countries, the army represents the chance of moving up the social scale or getting a secure job based on corruption and risk-avoidance.

The police represent the main anti-insurgency organization, particularly in the towns. Their skill, especially at the beginning of the insurgency, is an important factor. As for the judicial system, it is brought into line with the demands of the situation. In democratic countries, there is an independent authority to monitor any such changes.

It is useless for a counter-insurgency to try to imitate the guerrilla movement's political strategy. It is better to make effective use of the superior means at its disposal. For political and social reasons, for example, the counter-insurgency may not be able to carry out some of the reforms called for by the adversary and whose introduction would have deprived the guerrillas of part of their support among the population. The counter-insurgency will get quicker results if it tries both to infiltrate the guerrilla movement and to strengthen the machinery of repression (even without introducing reforms).

Infiltration pays off handsomely at the very start of a movement, when it is still numerically weak. But it becomes far easier a little later, when there is wide-scale recruitment (at the beginning, people are co-opted). It needs only one informer at the right level. Playing on a movement's internal contradictions (as long as they are known) by manipulating even a small fraction can also prove effective. A good example is Amilcar Cabral, assassinated in 1973 by members of his own party who had been manipulated by the Portuguese. (The Black Guineans had been promised independence on condition that they got rid of the half-caste Cape Verdians.)

In political terms, a counter-insurgency seeks to divide the adversary's support base. Ethnic, religious, linguistic, regional and social differences or antagonisms are played on to reduce the guerrilla movement's social base. The entire history of the colonial conquests is based on the use of local antagonisms. Far from having disappeared in the age of modern nationalism, there are many countries where 'ethnostrategies' could still be made use of. In this respect, the Soviets in Afghanistan are remarkably well served by the traditional societies they are trying to put down.

As to social factors, if the conflict hinges on the class struggle, it is easy to win over or neutralize relatively large social strata. This political work is carried out in addition to active military operations, and is accompanied by the selective liquidation of opponents. In practice, these liquidations are mostly indiscriminate.

Natural obstacles such as mountains, forests, jungles, marshland and boscage are a help to the guerrillas. The role of counter-insurgency is to create obstacles for the guerrilla movement. This was the case with the triple wall built by the Moroccan forces (1978-84) in the Western Sahara against Polisario, and the line of electrified barbed wire fences built by the French along the Moroccan and Tunisian frontiers during the Algerian war. Such obstacles are undoubtedly effective. They prevent access to the sanctuary — or considerably reduce its importance — and force the guerrillas to withdraw (when the terrain is suitable) into the country offering sanctuary. In the case of Afghanistan, given the nature of the country and the length of its borders with Pakistan alone, the simplest and most economical solution for the Soviets would be to persuade Pakistan to end its logistical support for the insurgents.

The counter-insurgency tries hard to locate and destroy the routes normally used by convoys, and to force the adversary to use other more difficult access routes that will slow down the flow of supplies. The counter-insurgency must see to it that any penetration operation by the guerrillas is costly; every day-time march must involve great risks, especially when convoys or large groups are involved. In military terms, the counter-insurgency uses airborne pursuit whenever possible.

When the guerrillas hold a particular region and decide it is worth fighting a battle to hold onto it, the counter-insurgency can make this defence very costly: any frontal attack may be turned to the advantage of the counter-insurgency, given its superior firepower and numbers. Nevertheless the nature of the terrain, the knowledge each side has of it, and the motivation of the combatants may make the outcome of the battle uncertain.

Contrary to a widespread belief, time is not necessarily on the side of the guerrillas. While the time factor may be vital in order for the weaker side gradually to build up strength, it is not enough just to let time pass. Time belongs to those who can put it to productive use. Moreover, the counter-insurgency also needs time: time to reorganize the administration, the police and the army in line with a war situation, time to comb areas and gather intelligence, time to try and dismantle the adversary's underground political infrastructure, time to bleed the insurgents' forces though carefully prepared offensives.

An offensive that seizes control of territory held by the adversary and causes it major losses is in itself an excellent result for the army. But it is not enough. Once a zone has been 'cleared', the army usually leaves it since it cannot hope to hold every zone in the country. The insurgents may return and find enough support among the population for them to rebuild what has just been lost. In many guerrilla wars, a continuously deteriorating situation in zones that have to be 'pacified' time and again is one of the most debilitating consequences for the army.

It is the population that is at stake. If the army cannot win the population over, it tries at least to control it. In this case, it relies on an active minority favourable to the state. This implies that the risk run by such elements is not too great; otherwise they would be systematically eliminated by the insurgents.

If the state judges it impossible to win the support of the population — though it is always possible to have the support of part of it, for ethnic, religious or social reasons — there are other methods available. Forced resettlement in the rural areas is one such tactic. Though it is a tricky process, it has proved its worth, both where it has succeeded and where it has failed: it produced positive results in Malaya and Guinea-Bissau and negative ones in Vietnam. Everything depends on how the resettlement is carried out, and the efficiency of those responsible — it is a great blow for a population to leave its village. The new hamlet should offer both a sense of security and a distinct improvement in well-being. If resettlement comes too late, after the adversary has already established his underground political organization (as in South Vietnam), then it is pointless. If the population is large, these resettlement areas often resemble vast internment camps, with their mass distribution of medicine and soup. The first resettlements of this type in modern times date back to the Spanish counter-insurgency in Cuba, carried out by General Weyler (1895-98), and the British concentration camps set up by Kitchener during the Boer war (1899-1902), where 60,000 women and children perished.

The 'production of refugees' is one of the classic tactics of counter-insurgency. These refugees can be directed towards the towns (Saigon's population rose from about 1 million to almost 4 million between 1965 and 1973) or they can be forced to leave the country (some 3 million Afghan refugees, especially from the south-east, have fled to Pakistan over the last five years).

One of the counter-insurgency's major tasks is to prevent the insurgents undertaking political organization at the base. At the same time, the army may introduce reforms in an attempt to win over or neutralize the population. Political action is preceded by military operations intended both to force the insurgents out of the region and to demonstrate the army's strength and its determination to occupy the area permanently. Such a policy is only viable in zones selected as favourable, whether socially or geographically, to the government forces.

The various stages in the counter-insurgency depend on the nature of each situation. In general, the most important tasks are the following: gathering intelligence; harassing the adversary as soon as he is located; destroying or reducing his logistic resources; controlling the population and providing reasonable living conditions for them; destroying as far as possible the insurgents' underground political infrastructure; concentrating sufficient forces to destroy the bulk of the enemy forces; and playing on every possible division, including those within the insurgent movement itself.

A counter-insurgency may seize the initiative by selecting the time and place it will strike while taking advantage of the element of surprise — as with airborne operations against bases or regions held by the insurgents. The important thing is to leave as little respite as possible after the offensive has been launched.

Once the insurgent forces have been driven out of a given zone, measures are taken to prevent their return: garrisons are established to patrol and keep a watch on the population; agents of the insurgency are identified and eliminated. This process is then repeated in other zones so as to reduce to a minimum the regions held by the insurgents. Operations will be co-ordinated throughout and the supremacy of the political over the military maintained, even if decisions are taken at the local level when circumstances demand.

If the counter-insurgency is fighting a conventional guerrilla movement that has not yet established a true partisan army, the regular army's mobile units need only light, mobile forces backed up by helicopters. The army generally has the advantage of a telecommunications system that leads to increased mobility and effectiveness. The most difficult thing appears to be to adapt to this kind of warfare.

When conditions allow, the army attacks the insurgents' strongholds. A defeat on the ground may demoralize the adversary and above all show the population that, in military terms, the army is stronger. But it is better for the army to attack a less securely held region than to suffer a defeat, since failure has the opposite result: it strengthens the adversary's morale and gains the respect of the population. The army too needs time and experience in order to be truly operational: it must adapt to the terrain and to the new circumstances of guerrilla warfare. No one operation is decisive: what counts, in the long run, is to break the offensive capacity of the guerrilla movement and wear it down. The army must see to it that the guerrillas are as much as possible on the defensive, or better, are repeatedly put to flight. Once a region has been invested by mobile units, it is controlled by units stationed there. Ideally, the army should avoid committing excesses and remember that it represents not only a striking force but also law and order. Any excess must be punished in public and all damage must be repaired. A soldier must not steal or rape. Otherwise, all attempts at creating better conditions in the region (whether on the medical, educational or economic level) will fail. Control of the population also means protecting those who co-operate with the army. The best propaganda consists in finding concrete solutions to everyday problems in the village or region, wherever possible. With tenacity, will and determination, experience shows that a counter-insurgency can win.

Chaliand '87: 77-84.

4
Terrorism

In 1968, the year the PFLP hijacked an El Al plane and forced it to land in Rome, a new type of terrorism was born: transnational terrorism, whose main purpose is propaganda. This political terrorism has developed rapidly. It cannot be understood in isolation from the ideological context that has helped to produce it and without some appreciation of the development of communications and the media.

The word terror has its political origins in the French revolution — in the sense of terror carried out by the state. With the Enlightenment, the idea of popular sovereignty was born: it was in its name and in its defence that the revolution justified state terror. Political terrorism was later used in the second half of the nineteenth century, notably by the Russian populists who were influenced by the Romantic tradition. The distant origin of terrorism is to be found in tyrannicide. The assassination of a tyrant was traditionally committed in the name of justice. But it was in the name of ideological purity that the most powerful terrorist organization ever created, that of the Assassins,[1] operated in the eleventh and twelfth centuries.

In today's world, after the ideas introduced by the French revolution, Romanticism, socialism, and so on, the doctrine of just rebellion[2] no longer meets with strong objections; it has become a widespread phenomenon. Over the last four decades, the right of peoples to self-determination, at least when under colonial domination, has become a driving force. Up to the Second World War the prevailing ethos was a sort of conservatism based on law and order in the colonial empires; after the war this gradually collapsed. Since the early 1960s, a 'Third Worldist' ideology has sanctified the idea of rebellion. It is here that the systematic recourse to violence has its roots. In a despotic system where the punishment was death — with or without trial — terrorism was a last resort. It has now become a means of getting one's voice heard, with very limited risks, at least in democratic countries. The frequent resort to terrorism can also partly be explained by the extraordinary development of the media. Mass communications, particularly in the audiovisual domain, have come to play an important role for terrorist organizations since they regularly broadcast their activities. This is one of the major characteristics of contemporary terrorism. The other characteristic feature is the transnational dimension — though not new in itself, its use has never before been as systematic. It too derives from the development of communications, notably by air.

Modern terrorism can be dated back to the Russian populists, the Narodniks, who were active between 1878 and 1881. Vera Zasulich brought down the St Petersburg government after a trial of the populists. The following year was marked by a failed attempt on the life of the Tsar. For the Narodnaya Volya, the attacks were aimed at overthrowing the Tsarist tyranny.[3] In 1881 the Tsar was assassinated, but this did not mean that the Tsarist tyranny had been overthrown. The terrorism of the populists was nevertheless the expression of the general crisis in Russian society. It should be noted that the populists published a statement condemning the use of terrorism in democratic countries when the American president James Garfield was assassinated in 1881. A new wave of assassinations broke out in 1902. This time, however, rather than being conceived of as an isolated event, the Social Revolutionaries used it as an adjunct to the revolutionary potential of the masses.

Nihilist and anarchist schools of thought also advocated and practised terrorism in the nineteenth century. Nechayev[4] and Bakunin were its principal ideologists, as well as Kropotkin, who saw terror as a means of awakening the spirit of revolt among the masses.[5] In 1881 an Anarchist International was set up in London, while the 1880s saw numerous attacks,[6] particularly in France (by people such as Ravachol, Auguste Vailland and Emile Henry).

It should be noted that terrorism played virtually no role for Marx and his circle, since violence was seen as collective. With the Commune, the model became the urban uprising. As a phenomenon, modern terrorism was active in Europe (and in the United States, where President McKinley was assassinated in 1901) between 1878 and the First World War. Later, it was increasingly used by the Fascist Right.

In the framework of national-type struggles, three movements resorted to a more classical use of terrorism: the Armenians in the social democratic Dashnak Party (who seized the Ottoman Bank in Constantinople in 1896); the Macedonians in IMRO[7] from 1893 to 1934 (and particularly after the First World War); and the Irish. By seeking to provoke a response from the Ottoman empire, the Macedonians and the Armenians tried to get the European powers to intervene on their behalf. But this strategy, adopted from the Bulgarian model which had led to Bulgaria's independence in 1878, failed to produce the expected results. The Irish demand for home rule was accompanied by all forms of violence as early as the 1850s; and in the wake of the First World War it was finally successful, with the exception of Northern Ireland. A breakaway faction of the IRA fought the Irish army during the 1920s and 1930s, using terrorism and sabotage. Their example was to be copied.

As for the counter-revolutionary Right in the 1920s and

1930s, it included among others Cornelius Codreanu's Iron Guard in Romania, Ante Pavelich's Ustachis in Croatia and other Fascist leagues.

The use of terrorism and sabotage during the Second World War is well known. After the war, terrorism was extensively used by two minority organizations in Palestine: the Irgun Zvai Leumi (National Military Organization), founded by the right wing of the Zionist movement and led by Jabotinsky and Menachem Begin; and the Stern Gang,[8] which was an extremist offshoot of the Irgun. The majority of Zionist leaders thought that the Haganah, a self-defence organization, was sufficient.

One of the few movements to use terrorism systematically (while resorting to a combination of guerrilla ambushes and terrorist actions, including sabotage) was the Cypriot EOKA (1954–57) led by General Grivas. The Irgun and EOKA drew their inspiration from the methods used by the Irish before the war. Both movements were to achieve their aims: Britain withdrew from Palestine and Cyprus.

Today a whole range of movements, groups and sects are ranged under the heading terrorism. It may therefore be helpful to draw up a typology:

1. The first group is comprised of liberation movements[9] with a popular base, a political leadership and armed forces: terrorism in general is not the main feature of these movements. In the classical tradition, terrorism is only a specialized branch within the armed forces or one of the activities, often a minor one, of the combatants. This terrorism may be rural or urban. The NLF in South Vietnam, for example, used terrorism to liquidate agents of the Diem government in the villages. In the towns, specialist groups used sabotage and terrorism (such as the murder of army officers and policemen). The Algerian FLN frequently resorted to terrorism: the liquidation of agents of colonialism; intimidation of the

population to establish the movement's control; liquidation of rival movements; and indiscriminate terrorism to split communities along ethnic lines. As already mentioned, the Irish, the Zionists and the Greek Cypriots all made extensive use of terrorism. Nevertheless their organizations had social depth, a political leadership and an overall strategy capable of attaining an objective and altering the situation on the ground.

Liberation movements with an ethnic and/or religious character, and movements aiming at self-government or independence and which have a mass base, fall into this first category. Thus the Palestine Liberation Organization (PLO) belongs here, as does the IRA, since both movements use essentially terrorist-type actions.

Given the particular climate of violence and secrecy that terrorism involves, factions within a movement often reject the realistic or moderate platform agreed to by the political leadership. This was the case of the Irish IRA members immediately after Ireland (Eire) gained independence. Today it is true of a faction of the Basque ETA which rejects the status of autonomy and demands independence. As a grotesque imitation of a liberation movement, mention might also be made of the Corsican elements of the Corsican National Liberation Front. The fate of these small groups may vary, but in general they end up marking time or are gradually liquidated unless the movement destroys itself as a result of internal crises born of the impasse.

Very few movements have won decisive political successes through an exclusive or preponderant use of terrorism. After the Second World War, the only examples are Palestine, Cyprus and Aden (1964).[10] In each case, however, there was a national movement with broad support, whether direct or indirect. In these cases, therefore, terrorism acted as a substitute for guerrilla warfare since it was better adapted to the conditions and potential of both the situation and the movement itself. From 1960 onwards, the Algerian FLN's campaign of urban terrorism was the direct result of the crushing of the *wilayas'* offensive capabilities.

In this sense, the PLO uses terrorism because — apart from commando operations conducted mainly from Jordan in 1968-70, and subsequently from Lebanon — it has been unable to hit the adversary in any other way. Terrorism has increasingly become a political propaganda weapon: it is more important to gain publicity for the movement and prevent it slipping into oblivion than to strike a blow at the adversary.

2. The second category covers anti-imperialist or revolutionary groups without a mass base, often based on the class struggle, and giving pride of place to armed struggle in the almost exclusive form of terrorism (urban guerrilla warfare) in non-democratic countries. Among the Latin American groups, the Marighella group in Brazil, the Tupamaros in Uruguay and the Montoneros in Argentina are examples of this kind of movement. The tiny far-Left Turkish groups of the 1970s and the *fedayeen* and *mujahideen-e khalq* in Iran belong, to varying degrees, to this type of organization. Given the weakness of their social base, the action of these groups usually ends in failure; it results in the state becoming more repressive, and the rise to power of the most extreme elements such as the far Right.

Mention should also be made of groups of nationalist exiles or emigrés with demands that historical circumstances make it impossible to satisfy. This is the case of the small Armenian organizations that have been using terrorist means since 1975, mostly against representatives of the Turkish state.[11] In a different context, it is also the case of the anti-Tito Croatian groups.

3. The third category covers political sects whose aim is to bring about a revolution in democratic industrial societies. Over the last fifteen years or so, there have been several groups with common characteristics: the Weathermen, the Red Army Fraction, the Red Brigades, and so on. These are

groups without a social base; their strategy rests on the ideological assumption that the system is fundamentally oppressive. The violence carried out by these groups is designed to show the masses the coercive nature of the system; the masses are then expected to identify with the group, thanks to the new consciousness supposedly raised through the mechanism of the spiral of violence and repression.

Their very philosophy condemns such groups to failure — this may in turn encourage the emergence of nihilist fractions that no longer attempt to win popular support, and may end up using banditry simply as a means of existence. Extreme right-wing movements[12] (terrorism, like guerrilla warfare, has no particular ideological colour, but is above all a technique) may also operate in a democratic country. The chances of their having a serious effect on the country's political stability — unless there is a major crisis — are equally slim.

4. State or para-state terrorism constitutes the fourth category. This form of terrorism invariably causes more victims than propaganda terrorism, since its goal is not to be seen as a spectacular action, but to cause terror by liquidating (often on a massive scale) real or potential opponents. It is often the state itself that officially carries out this 'restoration of order'. Sometimes it is left to special units — 'death squads' were active in Brazil between 1969 and 1972, for example, whereas Guatemala had para-state units that, particularly in the years 1980-82, liquidated political opponents in the urban areas and massacred Indians in the rural areas. Repressive terrorism has always been the weapon of tyranny and despotism. Certain states also use specially trained commando units for occasional operations. The Israeli secret service assassinated three Fatah leaders in Beirut in 1973 in response to terrorist actions in Israel, and the French ambassador was assassinated in Beirut in 1982 by the Syrian secret services. Libya uses terrorism as a method of coercive diplomacy. We should also mention the attempted

assassination of Pope John Paul II in 1982 by a Turkish agent manipulated or used by the Bulgarian secret services.

Mention must also be made of the use of torture by numerous states. According to Paul Wilkinson, one of the best British experts on terrorism, torture is the ultimate form of individualized terror. Conversely, in Iran, for example, we are witnessing a phase of terror based on religious ideology, truth being decreed by the mullahs.

After the repeated failures of rural *focos* and the death of Che Guevara in Bolivia in 1967, Carlos Marighella attempted to develop a new strategy which, in the long run, would integrate urban and rural guerrilla warfare. He only had time to start elaborating an urban guerrilla warfare strategy. It consisted, according to Marighella, in 'converting the political crisis into armed struggle by means of a series of violent actions that would force the government to transform the country's political situation into a military one'.

Marighella calculated that, by inducing the authorities to act repressively, the blame would fall on the state. In practice, however, this repression had the effect of dismantling the revolutionary organization without leading to anything more than passive support from the masses. And even then, the organization would have had to calculate the potential support for such actions among the population: needless to say, there is a big difference between sympathy and active support.

Indeed, Marighella himself saw the contradictions in his strategy. Among the 'seven deadly sins' of the urban guerrilla he mentioned in his 'Minimanual' are:

> Over-valuing the urban struggle: those who are wholeheartedly absorbed in the excitement of guerrilla activity in the towns may give too little attention to launching guerrilla fighting in the countryside. They may come to think urban fighting is decisive, and devote all

their organizing powers to that. Towns can be strategically encircled, and then we can only evade or break the cordon if there is guerrilla activity in the country as well. Without that we are always open to severe damage from the enemy...[13]

In practice, the Marighella strategy of the 'urban guerrilla' suffers from several intrinsic weaknesses: the lack of organized popular support, given the movement's clandestine nature and the fact that it involves very few people; and the assumption that the state is weak or has already been weakened — which was not the case with the Brazilian state, a military dictatorship since 1964. Despite his rejection of the strategy of the rural *foco*, Marighella's 'urban guerrilla'[14] was, in fact, an urban *foco*.

In Uruguay, the Tupamaros rightly saw the capital Montevideo as the strategic centre, given that half the country's population was concentrated there. The towns made it impossible to use air power and artillery — at least in the framework of counter-terrorism — which deprived the adversary of some of his advantages. Uruguay is 80 per cent urbanized, and the rural areas (essentially the plains) could only act as a diversion to reduce the pressure of the armed forces in the towns. For the Tupamaros, Montevideo, like all large cities, offered a number of advantages. There were ready-made targets within easy reach: embassies, administrative buildings, businessmen, media, banks.

The Tupamaros experienced an initial period of euphoria, with successful operations that were both spectacular and virtually without casualties, and won them the sympathy of part of the population. It must be stressed, however, that the Tupamaros were not at the time fighting an anti-democratic government. They maintained that the increase in terrorist acts would unmask a government based on oppression, but it merely led to the rise of the far Right. As time passed, sympathetic public opinion grew weary and reacted less and

less favourably to the Tupamaros' operations. The movement — which had a few thousand members and relied on
a network of friends and accomplices — gradually realized
that it was using violence as a substitute for public support.
Once again, the '*foco*-ist' character of the organization was
apparent, precisely when it was no longer sympathy that the
movement needed, but organized support. Like Marighella's
Brazilians, the Tupamaros in Uruguay faced the dilemma of
all small clandestine armed organizations: how to build a
political infrastructure when all the militants are mobilized
for military tasks. With hindsight, it appears that the
Tupamaros had made very few inroads among the masses,
the urban proletariat and the peasantry, even as regards recruiting them into the movement. In 1971-72 their attempts
to establish rural bases to loosen the grip on the cities ended
in failure. Their strategy consisted in provoking the authorities to overreact so as to win over the population. Yet
this was shown to be a dangerous game in which the state
— unless it is very weak — usually has the upper hand.

Like the rural guerrilla, the urban guerrilla is first and
foremost a political animal and his goal is to win over and
organize the population. It is a task that is generally seen as
secondary by small organizations obsessed by secrecy and
the need to carry out successful operations and observe their
impact on the media. Carrying out operations and ensuring
the movement's safety may even take up all the organization's
energy and limited forces. The population is above all a
spectator.[15] Despite a considerable effort to be selective, the
use of terrorism is ultimately counter-productive. Given the
lack of security, a sense of weariness replaces the initial en-
thusiasm. Once the element of surprise has worn off, admir-
ing comments on the efficiency of a successful operation or
one that has humiliated the forces of law and order change
to a blanket condemnation of violence.

In Uruguay the Tupamaros were crushed by the combination of determined, tough counter-terrorism in 1972, and

the rise of counter-terror on the part of the extreme Right. For the next twelve years, Uruguay was to inherit a tyrannical regime.

In the Third World, terrorism has been used as a technique of destabilization or as a (supposed) means of eventually seizing power. Yet in every case, as should have been foreseen, it has led to the rise of extremism.[16]

In totalitarian states such as the Soviet Union or elsewhere in Eastern Europe, the use of terrorism is rare. This is not because the necessary motivation or courage is lacking, but because people know in advance that the story will not be told. There was a recent new development, however, when the Bulgarian authorities admitted there had been a terrorist attack at Plovdiv in September 1984. Some terrorist acts have also been reported in the USSR. The impact of terrorism lies wholly in the stir it creates. Raymond Aron has observed that 'an action of violence is labelled "terrorist" when its psychological effects are out of all proportion to its physical result'.[17] In a totalitarian regime, terrorism is repressed without having produced its psychological effect.

In democratic countries, the media tend to focus on violent actions in a way that is out of all proportion to their political importance. Violence feeds on this to some extent, and terrorism and the media today form strange bedfellows. Of course, the reporting of terrorist actions is also part of democracy: but sensationalism, especially in its commercial form, is not necessarily the expression of democracy. Nevertheless the democracies, the usual targets of transnational terrorism (this is more true of Western Europe than of the United States), are less vulnerable than it might appear.

It is not true to say that terrorism destabilizes, or may destabilize, modern democratic states. It has not succeeded in destabilizing Italy, for example, which is still one of the least structured of all European states. The ideology of terrorist sects and the action of small terrorist groups operating on European soil do not represent a serious threat.[18] The mass base that could be won over by a national ideological sect is negligible or non-existent. As for transnational terrorism, it is almost always adopted because terrorism in a democratic country seems an easy substitute for guerrilla warfare back home. If guerrilla warfare is the weapon of the weak, terrorism is the weapon of the weaker still (excluding state terrorism, of course).

Terrorism was once used as a last resort, yet today (to use Walter Laqueur's words) it is seen as a 'means of expression'. This strategy — first adopted by the Palestinians — has been widely imitated by numerous groups all over the world. Having failed to win over Western public opinion,[19] the Palestinian commandos made the fullest use of the media to publicize the Palestinian national problem, a cause unknown to the general public before 1967-68. For the Palestinians, however, the use of transnational terrorism was also an admission of powerlessness. Terrorism soon became a substitute for a guerrilla war which, on the ground, never happened.

After 1968 the number of terrorist-type, particularly transnational, attacks increased considerably. Between 1963 and 1967, for example, only four planes were hijacked, whereas the number increased to fifty-five between 1968 and 1970. In 1971 sixty-one attempted hijackings were recorded, of which twenty-six, more than a third, were successful. In 1972 seventy-two terrorist attacks were made, half of which were successful.

Terrorism is perfectly suited to the means and capacities of underground movements with few members and no mass base. Whereas the PLO and the IRA enjoy popular support, many of the organizations active over the last decade have virtually none. Few contemporary terrorist organizations have more than 300 active members. The enhanced effectiveness of personal weapons gives small commando groups an awesome firepower, yet up to now they have usually made little use of it.

The actions carried out by various transnational terrorist groups cover the following: bomb attacks, kidnappings with ransom demands, aeroplane hijackings and the seizure of hostages, and assassinations, above all of diplomats and businessmen.

In ideological terms, a fair number of organizations and groups share a more or less Third Worldist, anti-imperialist rhetoric.[20] They have all, without exception, benefited from the aura of legitimacy bestowed on violence by the great anti-colonialist struggles of the 1950s and 1960s. However, any common goals implied by apparent similarities in statements or language are merely fortuitous or incidental. Each of these groups has its own local goal: whether Palestinians, Irish, Basques, Armenians, Iranians, Moluccans or Turks, they all have national or specific local objectives. Such groups are quick to imitate each other's methods, however, even if the movements have no formal organizational contact. Every innovation is immediately adopted.

Most terrorist-type actions have not resulted in a large number of casualties. Between 1963 and 1984 the bloodiest year for international terrorism was 1983, with 720 deaths, including the 241 US marines killed in a suicide attack in Beirut and the 57 American victims of the attack on the US embassy. If we exclude the victims of the Lebanese civil war[21] (who cannot be included under the heading 'victims of international terrorism'), we arrive at an average of around 200 deaths a year over the last fifteen years: there were 221 in 1982, for example (according to the Rand Corporation).[22] According to the US State Department, the number of victims of international terrorism between 1968 and 1975 was about 800. Whatever the differences in the two agencies' figures, the total number of victims between 1968 and 1984 stands at around 3,000 dead.[23] This is less than 15 per cent of the annual number of homicides in the United States (or a quarter of the victims of road traffic accidents each year in France). The use of terrorism — apart from a few particularly

horrifying indiscriminate attacks — has so far been relatively restrained. In the future, however, this is likely to be
less and less the case. When terrorism aims specifically to
cause victims, it finds the means to do so. The three suicide-
lorry attacks on American, French and Israeli troops in 1983
left almost 400 dead.

Relatively few attacks have caused more than ten deaths.
Among them are: the Japanese Red Army attack at Lod
airport (Israel) in May 1972: twenty-seven dead; the Munich
Olympic Games in September 1972: twelve dead; Fiumicino
airport (Italy) against a Pan Am plane in December 1973:
twenty-two dead; and Bologna railway station (Italy) in 1980:
eighty dead.

According to the CIA, the number of international terrorist attacks (which stood at around twelve a year between
1965 and 1967) increased as follows from 1968 to 1980:

1968	34	1972	157	1976	415	1980	642
1969	29	1973	127	1977	261		
1970	110	1974	344	1978	442		
1971	36	1975	276	1979	738		

There is a considerable difference between the CIA's figures
and those of the Rand Corporation. For the decade 1968–77
the CIA estimates the number of attacks worldwide at 2,698,
while the Rand Corporation, less involved in political manipulation, puts the figure at 1,022.[24] The Rand Corporation
also notes that of those 1,022 attacks, 729 caused no victims.

Thus it can be seen that the number of victims is not very
high. In addition, this psychological warfare costs the groups
engaging in it very little, whether in human lives, financial
investment or years in prison. Terrorist commandos run the
greatest risks in non-democratic countries such as Iran, Turkey or Ethiopia. According to the Rand Corporation, of 127
plane hijackings between 1968 and 1974, 10 per cent led to
the imprisonment or death of the terrorists. Between 1971

and 1975 fewer than half of those terrorists who were captured served prison sentences (thirteen months on average). It should be noted that one of the proclaimed aims of terrorism is to free imprisoned comrades, a solidarity which is understandable but somewhat lacking in political coherence: why refuse to be responsible for one's own actions?

Where and by whom are transnational acts of terrorism generally committed? In practice, terrorist attacks are mainly carried out in Western Europe, by far the most important theatre of operations. The United States and Canada lag far behind, as does Australia, no doubt protected by its geographical remoteness.

How can one explain the choice of Western Europe? Among the more obvious reasons are: freedom of movement; free access to the media, which give enormous publicity to acts of violence; public trials with due process of law; relatively light sentences (the death penalty has been abolished almost everywhere); and finally, the absence of torture,[25] which is not the case in non-democratic countries.

Compared to the United States, West European countries in general take a softer line on terrorism. The sentences laid down for identical acts are proportionately heavier in the US than in France, for example. American society itself is ideologically far less disposed to try to understand the motivation behind organizations that use violence. In fact, the United States has so far seen fewer attacks on its territory than Western Europe, Latin America,[26] the Middle East or North Africa. The regions that have recorded the fewest acts of terrorism over the last fifteen years are East Asia, the Pacific (including Australia), Eastern Europe and the USSR. The movements and groups engaging in transnational terrorism (along with states using terrorist-type methods) are almost all situated close to Western Europe — broadly speaking, in the eastern Mediterranean. Apart from a handful of Japanese, groups from East Africa and tropical Africa have virtually never resorted to transnational terrorism.

Given the weakness of the Lebanese state and its virtual dissolution, Lebanon between 1970 and 1982 acted as the gathering-point, training camp and sanctuary for most of these movements and groups: Palestinians, extreme left-wing Turks, Iranians, Japanese, Armenians, West Europeans, notably Germans, Italians and Irish, and so on.

It should be stressed that, so long as the major objective remains propaganda, terrorism does not represent a serious threat. But its use as an indirect strategy can become a much more serious affair, once states use or manipulate it. Propaganda terrorism is satisfied with publicizing its cause, reminding people of its existence and winning over public opinion — or at least that of its own community. As an indirect strategy used or manipulated by states, it becomes a significant means of coercion and intimidation.

In strictly military terms, terrorism has so far been relatively ineffective, although major advances in the area of personal weapons give the terrorists considerable firepower. It is no longer unusual to find a terrorist using an RPG-7 (40 mm grenade-launcher), a Soviet anti-tank weapon.[27] The IRA has also used the RPG-7 on various occasions. But there are more sophisticated weapons that may well be used by certain groups with the necessary contacts: the Soviet AT-3 guided missile-launcher which weighs only 12 kg and can hit a target at 300 m (or the American Dragon and Tow missiles). Shoulder-borne rocket-launchers, light mortars and MAC-11s (1,200 rounds a minute) are all part of the potential panoply of terrorist groups. It must be stressed once again, however, that indiscriminate terrorism has been rare and the various groups have generally shown restraint. Particularly loathsome acts like the seizure of children as hostages at Maalot (Israel) by the PDFLP have been isolated occurrences. Whenever indiscriminate terrorism has been used, this has usually led to internal crises or splits within the movement — as with the Armenian Secret Army for the Liberation of Armenia (ASALA) and the IRA.

European public opinion — traditionally less hostile to terrorism than American public opinion — has changed in recent years. The spectacular but abstract nature of propaganda terrorism has at first alienated and then angered people. Too many groups claiming allegiance to any old cause have mimicked the liberation struggle. States such as Libya and Iran have increasingly come to see the field of terrorism as a relatively inexpensive means of exerting pressure.

Violent actions in a democracy have a far greater impact than years of rural guerrilla warfare. What proportion of Western public opinion knew anything about the exemplary struggle waged by Amilcar Cabral in Guinea-Bissau from 1963 to 1973, for example? Throughout this extremely well-conducted liberation war, the most powerful Western democracies (the US, West Germany, France and Britain) supplied weapons and equipment to Fascist Portugal. How much do people know about today's most noteworthy armed struggle on the African continent, and indeed in the Third World — the struggle waged in Eritrea by the EPLF? The occasional article or report in the Western press usually describes it as a 'forgotten war'. The same is true of the Iranian Kurds' struggle against the Khomeini regime. Between 1968 and 1972 the Palestinians publicized their cause widely through transnational terrorist actions, but the lasting impression of many of these actions has been negative. The 1972 Munich Olympics ended in the death of the Israeli athletes and the Palestinian commando group that had taken them hostage. The operation could have been transformed into a political victory if the commando group, rather than setting conditions unacceptable to the Israeli state, had been content to ask for a few minutes' access to the media to explain its cause convincingly in exchange for freeing the hostages. But perhaps blood is necessary to make headlines.

The Western media's tendency to play up the sensational makes them appear to be participants in the violence, yet any attempt to block the broadcasting of such acts is anti-democratic. Indeed, the most damaging consequence for the democracies would be for terrorism to result in a reduction or ending of the freedom of the media. Moreover any restrictions on the reporting of terrorist acts might precipitate an escalation of violence in order to ensure coverage. Yet there must be a conscious effort not to create a mass psychosis and spread panic.

There is no 'international terrorist plot' co-ordinated in particular by the USSR, in the sense of a central body with a concerted policy, like the Comintern of years gone by.[28] There is ample evidence, however, of contacts, exchanges, *ad hoc* co-operation and direct or indirect manipulation by one state or another, notably Libya.

The most important area of co-operation is that of training, the major problem for most terrorist groups. From 1970 to 1982 Lebanon was the ideal training-ground, given the massive presence of the Palestinian movements and then the civil war. Numerous international groups were trained by the Palestinians, especially by the PFLP. Links were thus being formed[29] and methods of payment devised, as shown by the assassination of the Israeli consul in Istanbul in May 1971. In December 1975 a commando group led by the Venezuelan Carlos took the OPEC ministers hostage during their meeting in Vienna: the group included Palestinians and Germans. Some operations carried out on behalf of the Palestinians are the outcome of complex international dealings.

Countries such as Libya, Iran, South Yemen, Syria, Cuba and North Korea are more difficult to enter than Lebanon, yet they too have provided or still provide training and assistance for various international groups. The existence of such sanctuaries is vital, yet it is obviously difficult to estimate the scale of this assistance.

Despite advances in the fight against terrorism, the number of international terrorist operations has risen over the last ten years. The techniques have varied little. The most spec-

tacular — and most effective — innovation has been the use
of suicide-lorries loaded with explosives (Lebanon, 1983).
At present, the majority of operations are still concentrated
in Western Europe, particularly France.[30] In 1982 and 1983
there was a relative decrease in the number of attacks in West
Germany and Italy though 1984 saw a recrudescence in Italy.
It is clear that German groups (such as the 'revolutionary
cells') and the Italian Red Brigades have been heavily hit,
but not the right-wing Italian groups. The Palestinian groups
have also been affected by the Israeli invasion of Lebanon
and by the Syrian policy that precipitated their expulsion.
Yet the number and intensity of international terrorist activities have increased over the last three years. Despite the
fact that the bloodiest deeds have occurred in Lebanon in the
framework of a civil war, and that Western Europe tops the
list in terms of areas suffering from transnational attacks, the
United States remains the principal target. Not domestically
— where there are only some three or four dozen attacks a
year — but externally: American embassies, diplomats and
senior military officers are among the most frequent targets.
According to the Rand Corporation,[31] two-thirds of terrorist
activities in the US itself in 1982 and 1983 were the work of
Puerto Ricans, Jews, Cubans, Armenians and Muslims.
Puerto Rican groups attacked federal buildings in the name
of independence for their island. Jewish groups such as the
Jewish Defense League, Thunder of Zion and Hatikwa Leumi
attacked property belonging to the USSR to protest against
the treatment of Jews in the Soviet Union. Anti-Castroists
such as the Omega 7 group attacked firms doing business
with Cuba or Cuban representatives at the UN.

The Armenian terrorist groups (ASALA and the Justice
Commandos for the Armenian Genocide (JCAG)) attacked
almost exclusively Turkish targets. Finally, the Muslim
groups included both pro- and anti-Khomeini Iranians and
other nationalities.[32] The technique most commonly used
by all these groups was the planting of low-yield bombs.

At the international level, however, attacks have tended to be bloodier since the media naturally give more space to operations that result in casualties. The repetitive nature of a series of actions using methods already known to the public obliges the groups to strike harder or to innovate. Yet in essence the techniques are always the same: bombs, plane hijackings, the seizure of hostages, kidnappings and assassinations. Terrorism is feared more because of the threat of increasing manipulation by hostile states than because of the results obtained by terrorist groups so far. While terrorist methods undeniably paid off in colonial times (Palestine, Cyprus, Algeria), this is no longer the case. States cannot yield to blackmail by transnational groups, nor can they give in to the separatist activities of elements that are tiny minorities within their own communities (such as the Corsican National Liberation Front). At the European level, manipulation by other states — headed by Libya — is the overwhelming fear, especially if there is political infiltration. This may be directed at peace and ecological movements, or at Muslim immigrant workers (or their children), some of whom may be attracted by fundamentalism.

In this sense, terrorism represents a danger with considerable ramifications. Now that the colonial problem has been virtually settled, guerrilla warfare is undergoing a relative eclipse. We have yet to see, however, what new developments there will be in the field of terrorism. After the innovations of the early years (1968–75), terrorists have shown little imagination, but there is every reason to fear that they will be tempted, sooner or later, to attack the basic infrastructure of industrialized countries. The consequences would be so spectacular that they would not even need the media to report them. For the time being, however, terrorism is primarily limited (through the spectacle of violence) to psychological warfare.

5

Responses to Terrorism

Twenty years ago, on the eve of the 1967 Six Day war, no one could have predicted that there would be such an increase in the scale of terrorism. Since 1968 some fifty embassies have been seized and three heads of state or government assassinated: Aldo Moro in 1978, Anwar Sadat in 1981 and Indira Gandhi in 1984. Lord Mountbatten was assassinated in 1979, while a Turkish agent, certainly manipulated by the Bulgarians, almost managed to assassinate Pope John Paul II in 1982. At the same time as a long series of symbolic acts of violence, terrorism has had a major impact on international relations and within a number of states.

For the states concerned, terrorism poses costly problems of security: protecting political leaders, embassies, leading figures, and buildings that might serve as targets; watching airports; and so on. Several embassies, particularly those of the United States, have stepped up their security measures considerably. In Central America and the Middle East these embassies resemble fortresses.

What steps can be taken to counteract terrorism? The basis of any effective action (prevention, infiltration, neutralization, manipulation, liquidation) is intelligence. A file must be opened on each group, giving details of its social and political contacts: its suppliers of weapons, money and documents; its contracts; and its social network in general. There are two distinct aspects of intelligence: collecting information, which is the vital basic task and inevitably involves a significant number of false leads; and interpreting information, which is above all a matter of sociological and political analysis. This demands a knowledge of the adversary's ideology, organization, methods and potential. West Germany's regularly updated computerized files are seen as a model in this respect. In France the problem is not so much the obtaining of information as its circulation from one bureau to another. Together with the organization needed to respond adequately to a surprise attack, information remains the essential element in checking terrorism.

Terrorism initially took the democracies by surprise. Since 1972, however, they have started to engage more seriously in the fight against terrorism and to take the first tentative steps in co-operation. It has taken much longer for some states to decide on a tough response to a number of challenges.[1] This does not include Israel, which has been in the front line since 1968 and has no alternative but to refuse to negotiate, backed up by reprisals. The most spectacular Israeli operation was at Entebbe (Uganda) in July 1976, when the Israeli hostages on a hijacked El Al plane were freed in a daring operation by airborne commandos. Other Israeli operations carried out as reprisals have mainly consisted in bombing Palestinian camps. In October 1977 West Germany decided to act to free a Lufthansa plane diverted to Mogadishu (Somalia). The successful operation was carried out by German specialist forces backed by British experts. In April 1980, the British Special Air Service (SAS) carried out a successful assault on the Iranian embassy in London, which was held by anti-Khomeini elements. Generally speaking, however, this kind of spectacular action is rare.

Conversely, when it is known that a particular action is the result of state terrorism (as, for example, the assassination of the French ambassador in Beirut in 1982), it is normal for the secret services to respond by showing that the game cannot be played with impunity. The Israeli secret services have made particular use of this sort of message.

In addition to information-gathering and taking precautions to protect potential targets, the democracies have a relatively large arsenal of means at their disposal. Significant changes have been made to legislation on preventive detention, home searches, and so on. In Britain, for example, where freedoms have always been jealously guarded, existing legislation has been adapted to the new situation created by terrorism (notably Irish). The UK Prevention of Terrorism (Temporary Provisions) Act, enacted in 1974 and renewed with minor changes in 1976, provided for longer periods of detention, the entering and searching of homes and the deportation of suspects. Britain has banned the IRA. It is now illegal to aid the organization, and anyone convicted of having dealings with it is liable to deportation. The period of detention has been increased to forty-eight hours, but can be extended to five days with the approval of the Home Secretary. At airports and ports, the police may detain a subject for seven days — again this period may be extended if the Home Secretary judges the request acceptable.

Given the serious challenge posed by the Red Army Fraction, West Germany's anti-terrorist legislation is the toughest in Western Europe. It allows the administration to refuse to employ elements deemed 'undesirable' (*Berufsverbot*). From 1974 to 1978 the Criminal Code was amended to give the authorities the greatest possible latitude in the fight against terrorism: five years' imprisonment for those who form or participate in, to whatever degree, a terrorist-type association (Sections 129 and 129a of the Code of Criminal Procedure — hereafter CPC); three years for propaganda against the constitution, or against the existence and security of the Federal Republic of Germany (Section 88a of the CPC). Any lawyer suspected of endangering the security of the state is debarred by order of the Federal Court of Justice. If a judge deems it useful, any oral or written contact between a lawyer and his client can be prohibited for a period of thirty days, renewable (*Kontakt-Sperregesetz*) (Section 48 of the CPC). The police are empowered to search a whole building if they have reason to believe that a suspect is hiding there. (Section 1,031 of the CPC).

The dangers of anti-terrorist legislation aimed at 'suspects' are obvious. Under the cover of the fight against terrorism, an attempt can also be made to eliminate any 'undesirable' opposition. Everything depends on a country's democratic traditions and the independence of its judiciary. Britain has created a special unit, the SAS, for use in the fight against terrorism: the unit is designed to intervene effectively when the state decides to make an assault on a position held by a terrorist group. Other European countries have also set up or developed special units for this purpose (the *Bundesgrenzschutz* in West Germany, for example). In the past several states, notably in Europe, have concluded secret agreements with one terrorist group or other by offering relative freedom of movement in return for immunity (not always respected). Fewer and fewer deals of this type are now negotiated. The fight against terrorism is meaningless, however, if the state yields to blackmail by a group or movement and does not show firmness. That does not mean that it is necessary to adopt a stand of total refusal to negotiate, as Israel and the United States generally do. Discussion and negotiation do not necessarily mean abdication. With certain groups, it is possible to make deals at little cost and without loss of prestige. In general, however, what is non-negotiable (i.e. according to the demands and conditions set by the commando groups) must remain so.

Murderous blackmail methods are used by international terrorist groups such as the Arab Armed Struggle Organization (AASO), the commando group led by Carlos, and the Lebanese Armed Revolutionary Factions (LARF). An indiscriminate attack in September 1974 at the Publicis Saint-Germain in Paris left two dead and many wounded. The attack was designed to put additional pressure on the French government to release a Japanese Red Army leader from prison — it was a 'back-up measure' to the group's taking of hostages at the French embassy in The Hague. (The leader's subsequent release was claimed as a victory by Carlos.) In March 1982 the same group struck again, once more to secure the release of imprisoned terrorists: a bomb exploded on the Paris-Toulouse Capitol train, causing the deaths of five people. A month later, a booby-trapped car exploded in the rue Marbeuf in Paris, on the day that the detained terrorists came to trial. This time they were sentenced. On 31 December 1983 a bomb killed two people at Marseilles station; on the same day, another bomb on the Marseilles-Paris TGV (high-speed train) left three dead. Responsibility for all these attacks was claimed by the AASO (Carlos), as was an attack aimed at the French Cultural Centre in Tripoli (Lebanon). This time the blackmail was aimed at the presence of French troops in Lebanon.

The introduction of media restrictions, whether recommendatory or mandatory, is a sensitive issue. Alone among the democracies, Israel and South Africa, two states with a greater concern for security than others, have persuaded their media to tone down the coverage given to terrorism. It is not inconceivable that certain European states may in future suggest a policy of self-censorship. Finally, increased co-operation between states would seem necessary, especially at a West European level, where the relatively small geographical area enables people to move rapidly from one country to another. In 1977 the Council of Europe adopted a convention on the suppression of terrorism, which is an attempt to create a viable framework for this purpose.

During the 1970s Italy clearly lacked determination in its fight against the terrorism of the Red Brigades, and even more against that of the far-Right groups. This can be explained by the historical characteristics of the Italian state. France, in this respect, has a radically different state tradition.

Terrorism

While the French have entered into negotiations or shown clemency with regard to particular organizations, this has been a political decision rather than the effect of slackness on the part of the state.

A not insignificant number of American diplomats have died because the American government has stood by its refusal to negotiate. This rigid attitude can be counter-productive. It is possible — without making important concessions, losing face or appearing weak — to save a greater number of human lives. Negotiations can be a means of imposing one's will on the adversary.

Conversely, it is obvious that yielding to terrorist demands merely invites new demands. By kidnapping a succession of American, German and Argentinian businessmen, the Argentinian Montoneros and the People's Revolutionary Army (ERP) were able to extort almost $100 million between 1970 and 1973.

Negotiating techniques have been developed and per-fected; they are designed either to lead towards some sort of negotiations or, more often, to win time in the case of hostage-taking (in embassy sieges, plane hijackings, and so on). Unless it has been decided always to resort to force, it is not effective to embark on this sort of confrontation (which is often symbolic) without having something to offer, even if it is only at the psychological level. For example, the French state's attitude over the last ten years seems in practice to have been dictated more by the nature of the terrorist group involved than by its demands. The French have yielded only in exceptional cases. In 1969 the United States agreed to hand over fifteen Brazilian political prisoners in return for the freeing of an American ambassador. Even the Israelis have agreed to negotiate on two or three occasions. But the aim of negotiations generally has nothing to do with giving in. The state can propose one of three alternatives: safe conduct for the terrorists in exchange for the hostages; a political trial (a goal pursued by a number of terrorist groups);[2] or the offer of something the state is not actually prepared to grant, but which the terrorists will no longer be in a position to demand once they have surrendered.

A firm attitude by the state should go hand in hand with self-restraint[3] on the part of the media and a campaign to educate public opinion. The 'sensationalization' of violence by the media merely helps terrorism in its psychological war. Repeated viewings of spectacular violent acts have a contagious effect and encourage imitation: the peak was reached in France during the summer of 1984 when two young people tried to pass themselves off as a political movement in order to hold the state to ransom.[4]

During the 1980s states have greatly improved their overall capacity to respond to terrorism. In the long run, a number of terrorist organizations have been seriously weakened. In December 1983 the German police captured some of the leaders of the Red Army Fraction.[5] In Italy, the police have relied heavily on *pentiti* (dissenters from the armed struggle) to obtain information enabling them to dismantle a large part of the Red Brigades' cells (1982–83). The results have been much less convincing with regard to extreme right-wing terrorists, who appear to enjoy sympathy at very high levels of Italian society and the state apparatus. A repeat of the extreme right-wing attack at Bologna station in August 1980, the most murderous attack in contemporary terrorism (eighty dead),[6] took place in December 1984 on the Naples-Milan train (sixteen dead and over a hundred wounded). Although it is still not clear who was responsible, this attack may have been an attempt by the extreme Right to discredit the democratic institutions, seen by a section of public opinion as incapable of ensuring respect for law and order. It is possible that there will be an increase in the numbers of such despicable indiscriminate attacks. For the impartial observer, however, terrorism today is still not at a level that might destabilize Western societies. In its present form, it does not represent a serious threat. Indeed, it can be seen as only the most spectacular form of psychological warfare, in return for a very small investment by the terrorist.

In addition to the measures already adopted, two further lines of defence against terrorism must be developed. First, the public must be educated, particularly on television, in order to free them from a 'terrorist psychosis' and to ensure that they are psychologically prepared to deal with the phenomenon. Second, there must be more specialist units[7] capable of rooting out the small number of terrorists who are agents of other states whose true goal is destabilization.

This is relevant in view of the new alliance contracted in Western Europe by Action Directe (France), the Red Army Fraction (West Germany) and the Communist Combatant Cells (CCC) (Belgium). The aim of these organizations is to use assassinations and other tactics to fight NATO, and more particularly the European alliance which is itself directed against the USSR. Whether these groups serve the objective interests of the Soviet Union or are indirectly manipulated by the USSR is of no importance. The only response to this new challenge is to put such groups out of action.

6
Psychological Warfare

Revolutionary guerrilla warfare and propaganda terrorism
— a particular form of psychological warfare — have been
the current techniques of violence for almost four decades.
These are decades during which the industrialized nations,
sheltered from the danger of a nuclear conflict, have not had
to fight a war on their own territory.

Between 1945 and 1962 the values that underpinned, or
seemed to underpin, the legitimacy of colonial domination
were rejected, often by armed force. By 1973 — the year
that marked both the end of the Vietnam war and the beginning of the oil crisis — the spirit of the age had altered
worldwide. Throughout this period, however many rear-
guard actions the West fought (the wars in Indochina, the
Algerian war, the war in Vietnam), the Western industrialized countries enjoyed over a quarter of a century of
exceptional growth. The period also marked the beginning
of American hegemony, the rise in military strength of the
USSR, the political decline of Europe and the emergence of
the Asian and African states.

The period of decolonization ended, somewhat late in the
day, with the 1974 coup that swept away the Salazar regime
in Portugal, and the subsequent independence of Portugal's
African colonies: Angola, Mozambique, Guinea-Bissau and
Cape Verde. With Zimbabwe's accession to independence

in 1980 (soon, no doubt, to be followed by Namibia), an era had come to an end: the era of armed struggle whose success was assured, given that colonialism had become out-moded in its classical form.

In the colonial context of the aftermath of the Second World War, revolutionary guerrilla warfare played a funda-mental role as an indirect strategy intended to seize indepen-dence politically. For the rest, revolutionary guerrilla move-ments — with the exception of the classic case of China — have had only a limited number of successes: in Indochina, and in Cuba and Nicaragua. There is a long list of guerrilla movements, whether based on class struggle or minority nationalism, that have failed in their struggle against an inde-pendent state. Today guerrilla warfare is the most potent means of pressure available to armed minorities (ethnic, ideological or religious) in their fight against states that are determined not to yield to them. This is true of Polisario's struggle against Morocco's grip on the Western Sahara, the EPLF against the Ethiopian state, the Farabundo Marti front against the Salvadorean regime, the Shining Path in Peru, the Kurds in the Democratic Party of Iranian Kurdistan (DPIK) and the Komala against the Khomeini regime, and the Afghan movements fighting the Kabul regime and the Soviet occupation. As a means of applying pressure, it has been adopted by movements opposing avowedly Marxist-Leninist revolutionary regimes — examples are the US-backed 'contras' of various hues in Nicaragua and, before them, the Angolans in the National Union for the Total Independence of Angola (UNITA) and the Mozambicans in the Mozambique National Resistance (RNM or Renamo) supported by South Africa.

In today's world, the right of peoples to self-determination can be seen essentially as the right of colonized peoples to self-determination — on condition that no state opposes it (see the example of Morocco in the Western Sahara). Con-versely, apart from the handful of guerrilla wars that have resulted in military victories, only those struggles supported by a powerful neighbouring state have resulted in independence in the Afro-Asian world. (India's intervention in Bengal made possible the creation of Bangladesh, for example.)

Outside Indochina, no Asian insurgency movement has so far been able to win out against an independent state. (There are numerous examples: Thailand, Malaya, the Philippines, Burma, India, Iraq, Iran, the Palestinians, and so on.) The same observation applies to Africa (Zimbabwe, like Namibia, being counted in the colonial category). UN support for these struggles merely proves the point. In fact, what is universally under attack is European and Western domination.

The success of the anti-colonial struggles was due to the fact that none of these wars was seen as of crucial importance by the metropoles. As regards the ideological — or psychological — aspect of the war, the metropoles themselves were in favour of emancipation, there was a desire for independence among the elites in the colonies, and the era of nationalism had arrived. The strength of nationalism (whether or not mixed with a dose of Leninism-Stalinism) proved to be decisive.

The great wave of decolonization drew to an end in the mid-1970s and marked the physical withdrawal of Westerners from a large part of the Asian and African world. It was a period characterized by a bad conscience, initially among a section of the intelligentsia in the colonizing countries, and then spread among public opinion at large. Given the evolution in ways of thinking among the colonized elites, and then the struggles waged in the name of national liberation, Europe appeared to be in flagrant contradiction with the very principles it claimed to incarnate: the right of peoples to self-determination and, in general, the ideals of freedom. This false position undermined the very foundations of a previously unshakeable imperial consensus. From an ideological and psychological point of view, it partly explains the political weakness of a Europe already drained by the Second World War. During the period 1965-73 the United States, though still the world's leading military power, suffered from a similar malaise in Vietnam.

The Cold War was above all (with the exception of the Korean war) fought at the ideological-psychological level. It was under Khrushchev, once the Cold War was over, that aid to liberation movements was first used systematically as an indirect strategy to weaken the adversary. After the Suez crisis of 1956, a new Soviet strategy began to take shape.[1] Positions were consolidated in Central Europe, seen by the Soviets as an essential buffer. The Korean war removed the epicentre of the East-West crisis from Europe. The USSR took note of the change in international relations symbolized by the Bandung Conference of 1955. This whole new strategy, based on support for liberation movements struggling against Western colonialism and imperialism, was finally endorsed (after several years delay) at the congress of eighty-one Communist Parties held in Moscow in December 1960. This congress was, moreover, the last to be held by the 'socialist camp'. The Sino-Soviet conflict, visible at one remove in Albania, became an official breach two years later.

From the second half of the 1950s the USSR was discreetly supplying aid to the Algerian FLN — though the amount was relatively modest compared to that given by Egypt and Yugoslavia. This was followed in the 1960s by a systematic policy of Soviet aid to a considerable number of movements: the Popular Movement for the Liberation of Angola (MPLA), the PAIGC and the Front for the Liberation of Mozambique (Frelimo), all struggling against Portuguese colonialism;[2] the South West Africa People's Organization (SWAPO) in Namibia; the ANC in South Africa; and so on. In the 1960s China sought to lead a new Third World International (the 'zone of storms'). It systematically but often clumsily supported all liberation movements opposed to those backed by the USSR.

Militarily, diplomatically and politically, this aid was designed to weaken the Western adversary, tie him down and nibble away at his positions, in short, to enjoy all the advantages of an indirect strategy. The most visible fruits of this policy appeared with the collapse of Portuguese colonialism, the move into Angola in 1975-76 and the coming to power of Frelimo in Mozambique.

Throughout the decolonization period and up to the end of the Vietnam war, the West was frequently on the defensive and was subjected to an intense campaign of psychological warfare. America's response during the Cold War was strictly Manichaean — quite an accurate reflection of Stalinist truths. During the period of so-called peaceful co-existence, and then that of *détente*, the USSR's most frequently used weapon was to make the adversary feel guilty.

This guilt feeling gradually disappeared in the second half of the 1970s. On the one hand, the age of great colonial or post-colonial expeditions had died with the end of the Vietnam war. On the other, the crisis that reached its peak from 1979 onwards occurred at a time of American withdrawal and major political setbacks: Angola in 1976; Ethiopia in 1977; the fall of the Shah of Iran in 1978; the Soviet intervention in Afghanistan in 1979; and the rise of Soviet military power during the 1970s. At the same time, many of the mobilizing myths of the 1960s were beginning to run out of steam, starting with the Chinese Cultural Revolution. In the West, the Solzhenitsyn affair gave the latest, but by no means the least effective, blow to this century's most obvious false illusion. Regimes like those of Pol Pot in Cambodia were denounced as aberrations, while in 1978 the brutal 'normalization' of South Vietnam by the regime in the North accelerated the departure of the 'boat people'. Imam Khomeini's theocratic regime, based on an intransigent and blinkered Shiism, strengthened the West's rejection of Islam and this type of revolutionary process.

During the Carter presidency, the Human Rights ideology

became an offensive weapon to be used against totalitarian and authoritarian regimes, especially if they were hostile to the West. The upshot of this whole process, which was at work between 1975 and 1980, was to bring to an end the American — and Western — guilt complex. One clear expression of this new mentality is the presidency of Ronald Reagan.

In 1983, when the issue of the SS20s blew up, the USSR sought to play less on Europe's guilt feelings than on its deep-seated need for security.

As already pointed out, terrorism used on its own is a substitute for guerrilla warfare; as such, it is the weapon of the weak. The various forms of propaganda terrorism have largely succeeded in drawing attention to themselves and the causes they are fighting for, but the only political success scored over the last fifteen years has been in the media. At most, it can be said that terrorist activities in Uruguay, Argentina and Turkey have succeeded in replacing democratic or semi-democratic regimes by dictatorships. The various terrorist groups that aspired to seize power have all been incapable of turning their actions into solid political gains. There have been the predictable failures of ideological terrorism in the industrialized countries: the Weathermen in the United States, the Red Army Fraction and other German groups,[3] and the Italian Red Brigades. Similarly, separatist struggles in states that are determined not to yield have been marking time: Northern Ireland, the Basque country, Corsica, and so on. Outside the industrialized countries, exclusively terrorist activities or activities limited to sabotage have been rare: the ANC, which engages in selective terrorism based on sabotage, carries out low-level activity in South Africa. In less than ten years the Armenian groups have killed twenty-six Turkish diplomats — or members of their families — and caused the deaths, in France, of two people in 1982 and seven others in 1983 in acts of indiscriminate terrorism (Orly group). These Armenian actions have been carried out in over twenty countries. According to the Rand Corporation, 'the scale of their geographic spread is equalled by no other group' (with attacks committed in Bulgaria [1981] and Yugoslavia [1982] which were the first terrorist attacks carried out in Eastern Europe). Yet apart from bringing to world attention the unacknowledged genocide of the Armenians from 1915 to 1916, the results — as was to be expected — have been zero. In fact, the declared objectives — the restoration or recovery of lands formerly occupied by Armenians in eastern Anatolia — would only have any meaning if these territories were still inhabited by Armenians.

As for the Palestinians, weakened once again by Israel's invasion of Lebanon in the summer of 1982, they have — as far as Arafat's wing of the PLO is concerned — been dealt a severe blow by Syria and the minority Palestinian factions it supports. Since 1983 Arafat's PLO has been split among several Arab countries, all at a considerable distance from the occupied territories. Terrorist activities are the only option left, apart from political negotiations including Jordan, a possibility the PLO rejects — which suits both Israel and Syria and perhaps even Jordan itself. In 1983 the PLO carried out only two attacks inside Israel itself.

Terrorism today is not the means to achieve a political solution any more than it was during the 1880-1914 period, when it was a technique of protest and a part of various ideologies such as populism and anarchism. Conversely, it remains the surest means of winning an audience in the age of the media and (Western) public opinion.

The requirements of clandestinity quickly cut off terrorist groups from the rest of the world and they often exist in virtual isolation. Thus they tend to be the victims of their own propaganda and often overestimate the potential impact and effectiveness of their actions. In the long run, their lack of a social base or any organization worthy of the name encourages one of two outcomes: either a progressive loss of contact with reality, or the adoption of banditry as a means of surviving as an apparatus (or the remains of an apparatus).

Over time, apart from a qualitative escalation of terrorism, the most serious danger is the indirect but systematic manipulation of terrorist groups, or the use of specialist commando groups by states exercising coercive diplomacy and persistently playing the role of trouble-makers. Together with Iran, Libya is the classic example of states that use this type of indirect strategy.[4] Syria uses it too, both in Lebanon and when dealing with the Palestinian problem.

The Universal Declaration of Human Rights and the concept of the nation-state represented a radical break in human history. Since then, the people — that is, the masses themselves, even though they are composed of an aggregate of the historical novelty known as the individual — have taken on a new importance. The entire political literature of the nineteenth century is haunted by the presence of the urban mob, whether called proletariat or populace.

It is Gustave Le Bon[5] who, at the turn of the century, deserves the credit for having understood and brought out the political implications of this mob irruption onto the scene. Modern propaganda aimed at mobilizing the masses found its true testing-ground during the first all-out war fought in the name of nationalist ideology on a Europe-wide basis: the war of 1914-18.[6] In the inter-war period its techniques were greatly expanded and refined by Fascism and Nazism on the one hand and Bolshevism on the other. In the Second World War the role of psychological warfare was even more important because the conflict had an ideological dimension.

The Cold War was merely the resumption of the ideological and psychological war between Bolshevism and the democracies or between Communism and Capitalism, briefly relegated to the background by the appearance of Hitlerite imperialism. With nuclear weapons ruling out direct conflict (for the time being), the entire East-West competition has been played out by means of indirect strategies such as crises (Berlin, 1948-49; Cuba, 1962) and their management, the use of guerrilla wars to weaken the adversary by challenging his hegemony (aid to national liberation movements)[7] and the manipulation, when possible, of terrorism (the attempted assassination of Pope John Paul II). Other strategies use all the resources of psychological warfare played out in the media, ranging from propaganda to disinformation.

Needless to say, this interpretation does not postulate that the liberation movements are agents of the USSR or that most of the groups using terrorism are being manipulated. The world may still be militarily bi-polar, yet aspirations for a political autonomy based on legitimate local demands or regional aims have influenced the *status quo* ever since the immediate post-war period.

However, underlying every confrontation, whether it be the spectre of a nuclear apocalypse (widely used in 1982-83), guerrilla wars or terrorism, the trial of wills is played out first of all at the psychological level.[8] This can be explained by the new importance of the masses and, in democratic countries, of public opinion. The masses have the dual characteristic of being sovereign (when they make choices by voting or when they influence decisions), yet also manipulable.

The ultimate dimension of guerrilla movements and terrorism, as of other indirect strategies, is played out in the mind, that is, in the political, that ambiguous domain where the skein of the rational and the irrational is inextricably entangled.

Postscript

The last two years have seen an increase in the scale of transnational terrorism. There were almost twice as many terrorist attacks in 1985 as in 1984, and the figure is still rising in 1986.

Of the regional groups, Indian Sikh terrorists caused the greatest number of victims in 1985, with the explosion on board an Air India passenger plane. There has been little change in the overall picture as regards the other regional movements that resort exclusively to terrorism (from the Irish and Basques at the top end of the scale to the Corsicans at the bottom). As for the Tamil movements in Sri Lanka, they do not rely on terrorism alone but also adopt guerrilla tactics.

Ideologically motivated European groups such as the Red Army Fraction, Action Directe and the Belgian CCC are still operating at a comparatively low level. One of the most active groups over the period 1985-86 has been the CCC, who took the Belgian police somewhat unawares. In Europe as a whole, however, including Italy, there have been very few such operations.

Transnational terrorism remains by far the most active form of terrorism. There has been an increase in both the number and the scope of such operations. Certain instances stand out over the past two years: the hijacking of an Italian cruise ship, the *Achille Lauro*, off the coast of Egypt by a

Palestinian commando group in 1985; terrorist attacks by Palestinian commandos in Karachi and on an Istanbul synagogue in 1986; attacks attributed to Libyan agents in both West Germany and Italy; and above all, two waves of attacks in France by Lebanese groups in February and September 1986.

There have been two new developments in the fight against terrorism. First, there was the US action against Col. Qadhafi in April 1986. Second, the European states, particularly France, have adopted tougher anti-terrorist measures and in general have taken a harder line.

The first major new development in the area of transnational terrorism has been the central role of Lebanese terrorism. The civil war there, with the accompanying fragmentation of society along confessional lines, the host of politico-religious ideologies, and interference by other states, has turned Lebanon into the ideal arena for the development of terrorist groups. Although there is nominally a Lebanese government, there has been no Lebanese *state* for the last ten years. Thus the country has become sanctuary, recruiting ground and crossroads for Middle Eastern transnational terrorism. In addition, it is in Lebanon that the two states which most frequently use terrorism as a means of coercive diplomacy are making their presence felt through intermediary groups or movements.

The various terrorist groups draw their inspiration from two main ideologies. On the one hand, there is the Palestinian nationalist current, notably — but not exclusively — the fraction backed by Syria. The distinguishing feature of such groups is their rejection of a political compromise such as Arafat's wing of the PLO might possibly be open to (and which implies, among other things, recognition of the state of Israel). This trend is not Islamicist, but Arab and Palestinian nationalist. The second trend is isolationist and characterized by a militant Islamicism. Its main support comes from a tiny minority fraction of Lebanese Shiites. It also counts a number of Sunnis among its ranks, however, since it stresses a politico-Islamic approach rather than Shiism as such. Various different fractions and groups come under its umbrella, including Islamic Amal, the Hezbollah and, to some extent, Islamic Jihad.

All these groups share a certain common approach: first, an anti-imperialist outlook that is fundamentally opposed to the West and all it stands for; and, second, an anti-Zionism that rejects both the state of Israel and the entire body of Western states that support it, whether directly or indirectly.

The Arab defeat in the June 1967 war led to a reassessment of the Palestinian question. The following year, the Palestinian movement was the first to embark on transnational operations; its example was soon to be followed by other groups. Islamicist groups have only really started to be active since the early 1980s, in other words, since the Khomeinist revolution. With the exception of the PLO — which is a political movement with a mass base, even if that base is fragmented — these new groups that have sprung up in the Middle East or eastern Mediterranean are fundamentally different from the national liberation movements of the 1950s and 1960s, in that none derives from a solid political party with an organized mass base. Almost without exception, they are small groups with self-proclaimed representatives. It is difficult to see, for example, who authorizes certain extremist, ultra-minority Lebanese groups to call for an Islamic, Iranian-style state in Lebanon.

The new factor in contemporary terrorism as compared with the national liberation movements (some of which also resort to terrorism) is the emergence of little groups with no organized links with the masses and no movement worthy of the name to draw up a political programme. There has been a massive increase in the number of minuscule groups which see indiscriminate terrorism as both tactic and political line. They no longer have a party or political commissar to keep an eye on this line or work on the relationship with the masses. The tiny Middle Eastern groups capitalize on a vague anti-Western sentiment but make no attempt to convince anyone of their ideology. In the past, the validity of a group's political line and strategy was measured in terms of its mass support. Thus, when put to the test between 1960 and 1967, the Latin American guerrilla groups based on the Cuban *foco* were shown to be a failure. Che Guevara's death was a clear illustration of his disastrous political analysis and military strategy.

Today there is no need to submit to any such test. A self-proclaimed grouping only needs to coin a few slogans and give itself some vague ideological clothing to feel entirely justified. The chaos and bloody feuding of the Lebanese civil war have led to an increasing spiral of violence among young people whose only prospects are 'group solidarity' and a programme of action based on elementary ideas that no longer even need to be explained to the people in whose name the groups are supposedly fighting.

How many Armenians, for example, identify with ASALA's militant anti-Western, Third Worldist, anti-Zionist line? In what way can this struggle by a handful of militants possibly concern the Armenian diaspora? It reveals considerable ideological blindness and lack of historical perspective for this Christian minority grouping — whose members are moreover neither Arab nor Persian — to believe that it might share common long-term revolutionary goals with movements based either on a militant Islamicism or on the most intransigent Arab nationalism, whatever the immediate general points of agreement.

Terrorist groups are becoming increasingly like outlaws, with their outright rejection of all rules not made by themselves. Why refuse to accept that the state has the right to imprison an individual who has used violence to kill? The guerrilla knows that he may be killed in action: the new brand of terrorist, on the other hand, protests at his 'unjust' imprisonment.

The Palestinian resistance is the last true mass national liberation movement in the Arab East. It is also the first that, from the outset and as a result of its progressive disintegration, has led to the appearance of small, non-mass-based groups backed by various states with an interest in manipulating the Palestinian movement. Egypt, Iraq and Syria, among others, have all had a hand in this state of affairs. Arafat's wing of the PLO has never managed to prevent or even control it. As a result, a wide variety of groups — including some from Europe and Japan — were freely able to receive training in Lebanon, where the Palestinians had set up a state within a state. From 1975 onwards, the civil war made conditions even more favourable for the development of terrorist groups.

The 1979 Iranian revolution has encouraged the rise of Shiism, and of militant Islamicism in general, in Lebanon and elsewhere. It has also led to the proliferation of terrorist groups and movements, all with small memberships but different ideological backgrounds. There is Islamic Amal, for example, which split off from Nabih Berri's Shiite Amal. Founded in 1982, led by Hussein Moussavi and with its main base at Baalbeck, Islamic Amal is close to the Iranians, but also has links with Syria. Then there are the Hezbollah, or Party of God. Also founded in 1982, they draw their inspiration from Muhammad Hussein Fadlallah, though they have no single uncontested leader. The Hezbollah have recently gained ground in Beirut, taking supporters mainly from Amal. Finally, there is Islamic Jihad, under whose banner operate various different groups, most of them close to Shiite Islam. (This does not prevent them having links with Syria, whose influence in Lebanon extends well beyond the areas under its direct control.)

As a general rule, Islamicism springs from the failure of nationalism and socialism, at both the Arab and pan-Arab level. Countries that have experienced a largely national, lay development process such as the Shah's Iran, Nasser's Egypt and Bourguiba's Tunisia are its most fertile breeding-ground. Elsewhere — in Lebanon, Nigeria or Malaysia — Islamicism serves, or is supposed to serve, as the ideological weapon that will topple non-Muslims from power or remove them from dominant positions in the economy.

As a political, social and cultural response by urban, frequently marginalized groups, Islamicism is characterized by a global rejection of the West and its value system. In political terms, the return to fundamental Islamic values can be seen as a rejection of existing constitutions, of institutionalized Islam and of those regimes that claim to draw their inspiration from Islam.

When one considers the local demographic and religious balance in Lebanon, though there may never be a return to the *status quo*, it is doubtful whether the groups that resort to transnational terrorism will be able to impose their extreme form of Islam.

Of all the European states, France has borne the brunt of transnational terrorism in 1986. Two waves of attacks in February and September 1986 left 10 dead and nearly 200 injured. The attacks were carried out by Lebanese Islamicist groups such as Islamic Jihad. Their stated goal was the liberation of three people held in French prisons, one of whom — Ibrahim Abdallah — is supposedly an important cadre and the person responsible for the murder of a US military attaché in Paris in 1985. In practice, however, the attacks were principally aimed at forcing France to alter its policy in the Middle East by reducing its military aid to Iraq and ending all interference in Lebanon. It is clear that French policy clashes with the interests of both Iran and Syria. Whatever secret negotiations may be in progress between the various parties, the situation created by the attacks cannot be allowed to force France to give in to the terrorists' demands.

The democracies have for many years treated terrorist groups as the relatively unimportant phenomena they actually are, with the media — particularly television — allowed to present terrorism as a reprehensible, if fascinating, spectacle. These countries have recently begun to take the issue more seriously.

Since 1985-86 co-operation between the democracies has moved beyond mere rhetoric, though we are still a long way from a situation where information and analysis circulate freely from one country to another. Checks and controls have been stepped up, particularly in France, and Italy is considering the introduction of electronic scanning of all diplomatic mail. But clandestine political support networks have been set up in Europe over the last ten years, and they will have to be dismantled if life is to be made more difficult for the external commando groups.

What has been the response to transnational terrorism used as a means of coercive diplomacy? The major event was undoubtedly the US bombing of Libya in spring 1986. Up to now US territory itself has been spared by transnational terrorism (a situation that might well change). Yet over the last two decades, it is America's interests and representatives that have been the principal target of the various terrorist groups.

It will be some time before the US bombing of Libya can be judged with any sort of objectivity. Since 1984-85 the Americans had sent out warning signals, threatening retaliatory action, the imposition of a boycott, the withdrawal of US citizens, the violation of Libyan airspace and what Libya considered its territorial waters, and so on. Each time Col. Qadhafi reacted by stepping up terrorist acts in West Germany, Italy, Britain... With a Republican president like Reagan, he should have expected a military response. The weaker side must always know where to draw the line. In the medium term, the Libyan operation has been positive as far as the US is concerned. Qadhafi has not carried out the reprisals he threatened in the wake of the bombing. The Libyan regime has been shown to be somewhat isolated in the Arab world. Apart from Sudan, there have been very few popular expressions of support for Qadhafi. Nor has the Libyan regime itself come out of it any stronger. As to the European states (which shortly before the US bombing had not dared to accuse Libya publicly of responsibility for a number of terrorist attacks), they subsequently condemned Libya by name at their Tokyo meeting. Of the three states that engage in terrorism as a means of coercive diplomacy (Iran, Syria and Libya), it should be noted that it was Libya that was attacked, not because it is the most actively involved in terrorism but because it is the most vulnerable.

All the indications are that transnational terrorism is here to stay: it has been shown to bring results at very low cost. Terrorism can be fought, even weakened, but it cannot be rooted out altogether. The democracies will have to learn to live with it.

The role of the media is to provide information, not to spread alarm. This is a psychological war in which the public has tended to overestimate the importance of terrorism and the European states to underestimate it. It is high time that every newspaper, magazine and television channel had one person responsible for all events connected with terrorism — someone capable of dealing with it competently and putting it into perspective. Terrorism is a political phenomenon; as such, it must be dealt with by political means.

There can be no unilateral, blanket condemnation of terrorism — unless one condemns all forms of violence, whatever the circumstances. Terrorism is always justified as a last resort. When up against the South African state, for example, what possible course of action is there other than a combination of political struggle (demonstrations, boycotts, sabotage, etc) and terrorism? Moreover South Africa itself is hardly in a position to condemn the (so far essentially selective) terrorism of the ANC when its own police systematically torture all suspects. State terror causes immeasurably more victims than individual acts of terrorism.

Nevertheless, apart from hitting the headlines, today's terrorist groups have made very few concrete political gains. The Palestinian question remains on the agenda — but its main strength derives from the physical presence of an overwhelming majority of Palestinians in the West Bank and Gaza in addition to a substantial majority in Jordan. Lebanon is embroiled in a civil war in which no one force has managed to come out on top, even if the *status quo* is gone for ever. In general terms, those states that have used coercive diplomacy based on terrorism have not won any political victories. The only undeniable and truly outstanding success has been the withdrawal of Western troops stationed in Lebanon in 1982-83, following the suicide attacks that killed 241 US marines and 83 French soldiers. The public's refusal to accept human losses in conflicts without any apparent advantage is one of the recent characteristics of the liberal democracies. It should be noted, however, that Israel — the state most threatened by terrorism for almost the last two decades — has not ceded anything of real importance or made any concessions.[1]

It is just possible that historians will see the Western media as having exaggerated the importance of the widespread use of terrorism from the late 1960s when compared with that of other hidden wars such as espionage.

Saint Jean d'Orléans
Quebec
October 1986

Notes

Preface
  1. G. Bonnet, *Les guerres insurrectionnelles. De l'Antiquité à nos jours* (Payot, Paris, 1958).
  2. G. Chaliand and J.P. Rageau, *Strategic Atlas* (Harper & Row, New York, 1984).

Chapter 1
  1. See the remarkable work by R. Emerson, *From Empire to Nation. The Rise to Self-Assertion of Asian and African Peoples* (Harvard University Press, Cambridge, Mass., 1960; and Beacon Press, Boston, Mass., 1962).
  2. General Douglas MacArthur was Supreme Commander for the Allied Powers.
  3. At the heart of these ideas lay concepts such as democracy, the critical spirit and the right to freedom of research.
  4. M. Rodinson, 'Marxisme et tiers monde' in *Marxisme et monde musulman* (Le Seuil, Paris, 1972).
  5. In 1864 a good third of Frenchmen did not understand French (E. Weber, *La fin des terroirs* (Fayard, Paris, 1983)). Cf. E. Kedourie, *Nationalism* (Hutchinson University Library, London, 1960).
  6. The US Declaration of Independence was couched (like other American statements) in terms of the natural rights of individuals, not in terms of the rights of nations as was usual in the nineteenth century.
  7. The Chinese Communist Party was founded in 1921 with twelve original members; a short-lived Communist Party was created in Egypt in 1921; the Vietnamese Communist Party was founded in 1925; and so on.
  8. Underlying nationalism is the assumption that the nation–state

is the way in which the world is naturally and finally to be organized. Nationalism also implies the idea, so redolent of the worst excesses, that the nation prevails over and above everything else.

9. Sun Yat-sen was a doctor, Gandhi, Jinnah and Bourguiba all lawyers, and Sukarno an engineer. Kenyatta studied in London, Nkrumah in the United States, Senghor in Paris and Nyerere in Edinburgh. The list is by no means exhaustive.

10. Woodrow Wilson said of the Empires of Central Europe that they ruled 'foreign peoples whom they had no natural right to govern'.

11. In the seventeenth century, being Protestant or Catholic was more important than whether one was French or Prussian.

12. On the psychological aspects of colonization, see A. Memmi, *The Colonizer and the Colonized*, trans. by L. Hoey (Orion Press, New York, 1965).

13. In this respect, the Declaration of the Rights of Peoples, proclaimed on 4 July 1976 in Algiers, is an altogether more advanced piece of legislation.

14. The last few years have nevertheless seen an increase in the number of (relative) democracies in Latin America.

Chapter 2

1. Camille Rougeron, *La prochaine guerre* (Berger-Lavrault, Paris, 1948), partly trans. in G. Chaliand (ed.), *Guerrilla Strategies. An Historical Anthology from the Long March to Afghanistan* (University of California Press, Berkeley and Los Angeles, 1982).

2. Food and fodder were purchased by the commissariat and paid for in cash.

3. Carl von Clausewitz, *The Campaign of 1810 in Russia* (John Murray, London, 1843).

4. Le Mière de Corvey, *Des partisans et des corps irreguliers* (Paris, 1823).

5. As well as the Greek war of independence (1821-29) and the Carlist wars of succession in Spain (1833-40).

6. Except the first Afghan campaign.

7. Of the 60,000 Spanish soldiers facing 3,000 Rifans, 13,000 died. See D.S. Woolman, *Rebels in the Rif* (Oxford University Press, London, 1969).

8. R. Pélissier: *Les guerres grises* (Pélissier, Montamets (France), 1977); and *La colonie du minotaure* (Pélissier, Montamets, 1978).

9. The only success was that of Ireland (1916-21), a European country fighting a democracy.

10. See Tukhachevski's article on counter-insurgency (1926) in

W. Laqueur (ed.), *The Guerrilla Reader. A Historical Anthology* (Wildwood House, London, 1978).

11. See E. Snow, *Red Star over China*, rev. & enl. edn (Penguin, Harmondsworth, 1972); and A. Smedley, *China's Red Army Marches* (Lawrence & Wishart, London, 1936).

12. 'Strategic Problems of China's Revolutionary War' in *Selected Works of Mao Tse-Tung*, vol. I (Lawrence & Wishart, London, 1954).

13. This is still the case in Afghanistan today, except for the organization in the Panjshir Valley and the zones influenced by the (Leninist) model adopted by Mahsoud, the leader of the Panjshir.

14. A. Cabral, *Unity and Struggle: Speeches and Writings*, trans. by M. Wolfers (Heinemann, London, 1980).

15. *Selected Works of Mao Tse-Tung*.

16. Cabral, *Unity and Struggle*.

17. See: D. Galula, *Counter Insurgency Warfare, Theory and Practice* (Praeger, New York, 1964); and B. O'Neill, W.R. Heaton and D.J. Albrecht (eds.), *Insurgency in the Modern World* (Westview Press, Boulder, Colo., 1980).

18. The Vietnamese revolutionaries did not claim to be a rebel organization like that in Cuba; given the country's historical traditions, they sought instead to incarnate legitimacy. They were fighting for the 'just cause', the others were soldiers of the 'evil cause'. Saigon's army, for example, was utterly corrupt. It pillaged, raped and behaved as a conqueror. The 30,000 American advisers allowed this state of affairs to continue, the policy being not to force their views on their allies. This led US troops into more and more fighting. According to W.R. Carson, a colonel in the Green Berets, out of 100,000 operations carried out by the army of the South, the 25th Division managed to make contact with the enemy on fewer than 100 occasions. (This is what was called 'search and avoid'.) See W.R. Carson, *The Betrayal* (Norton, New York, 1968).

19. See Chaliand, *Guerrilla Strategies*.

20. For many guerrilla movements in Asia, Africa and Latin America, this sort of aid is provided by three French organizations: Médecins sans frontières, Aide médicale internationale and Médecins du monde. They are doing magnificent work.

21. Another example is the Afghans, to a very large extent.

22. For the reasons behind the success or failure of the movements mentioned, see Chaliand, *Guerrilla Strategies*.

23. A *foco* is a mobile strategic base which launches the armed struggle without preparatory political work among the population and claims to lead by example. See the first critique of the *foco*:

'Révolution dans la révolution', in G. Chaliand, *Les faubourgs de l'histoire* (Calman-Levy, Paris, 1984).
 24. UNITA undoubtedly has a mass ethnic base in Ovimbundu country. On Angolan nationalism, see: J. Marcum, *The Angolan Revolution. Exile Politics and Guerrilla Warfare (1962-1976)* (MIT Press, Cambridge, Mass., 1978); and J. Stockwell, *In Search of Enemies. A C.I.A. Story* (Norton, New York, 1978).

Chapter 3
 1. R. Thompson, *Defeating Communist Insurgency* (Chatto & Windus, London, 1966).
 2. Needless to say, this rational calculation could not be made. The Algerian war occurred primarily because there had been settler colonization.

Chapter 4
 1. B. Lewis, *The Assassins. A Radical Sect in Islam* (Al Saqi, London, 1985).
 2. Although St Thomas Aquinas mentions it, the great dissenting voice in the West was that of Marsilius of Padua (in *Defensor Pacis*).
 3. There were other regicides in Europe at this time: there were attempts on the rulers of Germany, Spain and Italy in 1878; another attack on the Emperor of Germany in 1883; and in 1898 the Empress of Austria was assassinated.
 4. Nechayev published his *Catechism of a Revolutionist* in 1869.
 5. Many of the ideas current at that time have been taken up directly or indirectly today: despite appearances, the Red Army Fraction, better known as the Baader-Meinhof group, holds some of these views. In the same way, the Bakuninist idea of a revolution drawing on the support not of the proletariat but of the peasantry and thieves (a notion first put forward by Wilhelm Weitling, a disciple of Auguste Blanqui) was used by Mao Zedong and the Algerian FLN.
 6. Among the most important anarchists were Malatesta, Most, Fielden and Emma Goldmann.
 7. Up to the First World War the Macedonians adopted a mixture of guerrilla warfare and terrorism in their fight against Ottoman domination. Their national demands having failed to achieve anything, they then opted for straight terrorism, including transnational terrorism, against the Bulgarian state.
 8. The Stern Gang did not limit itself to selective terrorism: during the Arab rebellion of 1936-39 the gang threw bombs at Arab buses, markets, and so on. In the area of selective terrorism, however, the gang assassinated Lord Moyne, British Resident Minister in the Middle

East, in November 1944. The Irgun particularly attacked British military and administrative establishments; in July 1946 they blew up the King David Hotel in Jerusalem where the British headquarters were situated.

9. There are many liberation movements in which terrorism plays hardly any role: for example, the PAIGC in Guinea-Bissau; (Barzani's) Kurdish movement in Iraq during the 1960s and, since 1979, the Democratic Party of Iranian Kurdistan (DPIK); and the PFLE.

10. In Africa, the Mau-Mau was one of the few movements to make widespread use of terrorism.

11. A fraction of the Armenian Secret Army for the Liberation of Armenia (ASALA) has on several occasions attacked non-Turkish targets. It engaged in two criminal acts of indiscriminate terrorism in 1982 and 1983 (Orly group).

12. The French Secret Army Organization (OAS) at the end of the Algerian war is one example. Or, more recently, Charles Martel, Delta, and so on.

13. C. Marighella, *For the Liberation of Brazil*, trans. by J. Butt and R. Sheed (Penguin, Harmondsworth, 1971). [The Penguin edition adopts the spelling Marighela.]

14. Both Marighella and the Tupamaros were greatly influenced by the Spaniard Abraham Guillen (see 'Urban Guerrilla Strategy' and 'Assessment of the Uruguayan Tupamaros' in W. Laqueur (ed.), *The Guerrilla Reader. A Historical Anthology* (Wildwood House, London, 1978)). See also D.C. Hodges (ed.), *Philosophy of the Urban Guerrilla* (no pub., New York, 1913); and G. Chaliand (ed.), *Guerrilla Strategies. An Historical Anthology from the Long March to Afghanistan* (University of California Press, Berkeley and Los Angeles, 1982).

15. C.A. Russell, J.A. Miller and R.E. Hildner, 'The Urban Guerrilla in Latin America. A Selected Bibliography', *Latin America Research Review*, no. 9 (1 April 1974).

16. Turkey is a classic example of terrorism's lack of impact other than senseless chaos. The consequences were predictable: the coming to power of the military in 1980 and the establishment of a dictatorship to restore order.

17. Raymond Aron, *Peace and War* (Weidenfeld & Nicolson, London, 1966).

18. For them to represent a threat, the state would have to be seriously weakened by internal ethnic, social or other conflicts, or by a major economic crisis eroding the very values of democracy.

19. Conversely, they had won over public opinion in the Arab states.

20. Ideological differences exist none the less, and sometimes they

are very pronounced. Among the Armenians, for example, ASALA is influenced by Third Worldism, whereas the Justice Commandos for the Armenian Genocide (JCAG) have demonstrated in unambiguous terms that they do not share the prevailing anti-(Western) imperialism.

21. Who include almost 150 French and Israeli soldiers.

22. B. Cordes, B. Hoffman, *et al.*, *Trends in International Terrorism, 1982 and 1983* (Rand Corporation, Santa Monica, Calif., 1984).

23. This figure includes some 380 military victims of suicide-lorries in Lebanon in 1983, but excludes victims of local terrorism.

24. Cf. B. Jenkins, 'International Terrorism: Trends and Potentialities', *Journal of International Affairs*, no. 32 (1978), pp. 114-23.

25. It should be noted, however, that the IRA and ETA have, on several occasions, accused Britain and Spain of using torture.

26. The attacks here are local, not international.

27. The RPG-7 was first used during an attack in France in January 1975 by a Palestinian commando group (Black September) against an El Al plane. (It failed to reach its target and hit a Yugoslav plane instead.)

28. The reaction provoked by Claire Sterling's book, *The Terror Network: The Secret War of International Terrorism* (Weidenfeld & Nicolson, London, 1981) suggested as much.

29. In 1970 weapons stolen from the American Army at Butzback (West Germany) were used by the Red Army Fraction (Baader-Meinhof group); subsequently the same weapons were used by a commando group of the Japanese Red Army during the occupation of the French embassy in The Hague. There are many examples of weapons transferred in this way from one group to another.

30. Of the one hundred and eleven attacks carried out in 1982-83, forty-one were carried out by transnational groups (Iranians, Lebanese, Syrians, Palestinians and Armenians).

31. Cordes, Hoffman, *et al.*, *Trends in International Terrorism*.

32. The Rand Corporation notes that the remaining third of the attacks during 1982-83 were the work of Croatian separatists, Taiwan separatists, Filipino opponents of President Marcos, and so on.

Chapter 5

1. West Germany has reacted more strongly in the face of domestic terrorism than any other European state.

2. The penalties may be high. It is difficult to see why law-breaking, the use of violence or deliberate killing — in the name of whatever cause — should not involve the appropriate penalty.

3. In October 1977, when a Lufthansa plane was hijacked to

Mogadishu (Somalia), the commando group learned from the media that the captain was sending information to the authorities during routine broadcasts to the airport. It cost the captain his life.

4. In the United States, in 1971, D.B. Cooper did a parachute jump from a hijacked plane with a ransom of $200,000. Such is the impact of the media that five other people tried to use the same technique that week.

5. In January 1985 the Red Army Fraction announced that it would ally itself with the French group Action Directe, in particular in the fight against NATO.

6. This is true with the exception of the suicide attacks against the American and French armed forces in Lebanon in the framework of the civil war.

There had already been two other railway attacks in Italy: on the Palermo-Turin train on 22 July 1970 (six dead) and on the Italicus on 4 August 1974 (twelve dead). Among the numerous neo-Fascist groups are: the Revolutionary Armed Groups (NAR), Black Order, New Order, Rosa dei Venti, National Vanguard and the National Front.

7. The US has recently set up a spectacular anti-terrorist strike force, carried by nuclear submarines. The scale of the operation is no guarantee of the force's effectiveness.

Chapter 6

1. Stalin's attempts immediately after the war in Iran (Republic of Azerbaijan, 1946) or territorial demands on Turkey (Kars, Ardzhan) were rebuffed.

2. Portugal itself was supported by all the leading members of NATO: the United States, Britain, France and West Germany.

3. Such as the Revolutionary Cells (R2), or the *Umfeld*, close to the Red Army Fraction.

4. The USSR certainly had a role in the new offensive against NATO in early 1985.

5. G. Le Bon, *The Crowd: a Study of the Popular Mind* (Ernest Benn, London, 1947). The first French edition dates from 1895.

6. According to Mussolini, the 1914-18 war was the first in which Italians had fought together since the fall of Rome.

7. The US and some of its allies have adopted a similar policy with regard to the Afghan resistance so as to make the USSR pay as dearly as possible for its intervention. A kindness repaid in Central America...

8. What was above all an ideological war between East and West during the 1950s and 1960s is today, given the discrediting of Marxism-Leninism in the West, increasingly a psychological war (use of peace

movements, terrorism, disinformation).

Postscript

1. Can one use the word 'terrorism', on the other hand, when referring to the bombing of a civilian population carried out as an act of retaliation? It is a question worth asking. To the extent that it aimed to spread terror and thus destroy people's will to resist, can the repeated bombing of Dresden during the Second World War, for example, be described as terrorism?

Index of Names

Barzani, Mustafa, 58
'Basmachis', 41
Basques, 14, 81, 89, 110, 115
Batista, Fulgencio, 61
Begin, Menachem, 80
Beirut, 83, 89, 98, 119
Belgium, 104, 115
Bengal, 107
Berlin, 112
Berri, Nabih, 119
Bolivia, 84
Bologna, 90, 103
Bourguiba, Habib, 120
Brazil, 82, 83, 85, 86, 102
Britain, 21, 22, 27, 28-9, 30, 31,
    39, 40, 41, 60, 61, 62, 64, 68,
    73, 80, 84, 93, 98, 99, 100, 121
Buganda, see Uganda
Bukhara, 41
Bulgaria, 79, 84, 87, 97, 111
Burke, Edmund, 25
Burma, 28, 39, 107
Byzantium, 37

Cabral, Amilcar, 15, 42, 53, 70,
    93
Cambodia, 59, 109
Canada, 91
Cape Verde, 70, 105
Carlos, 94, 100-1
Carter, President Jimmy, 109
Castro, Fidel, 95
Caucasus, 20, 39, 40
CCC (Communist Combatant
    Cells), 104, 115
Che Guevara, 84, 118
Chiang Kai-shek, 12, 45, 67
China, 12, 20-30 *passim*, 37, 41,

43-5, 46, 56, 57, 60, 67, 106,
    108, 109
CIA (Central Intelligence
    Agency), 90
Clausewitz, Carl von, 12, 25, 38
Codreanu, Cornelius, 80
Colombia, 15
Comintern, 94
Congress Party, 31
Constantinople, 79
Corsica, 81, 110, 115
Corsican National Liberation
    Front, 81, 96
de Corvey, le Mière, 38
Council of Europe, 101
Croatia, 80, 82
Cuba, 12, 57, 59, 61, 73, 94, 95,
    106, 112, 118
Cyprus, 13, 80, 81, 96
Cyrenaica, 40
Czechoslovakia, 27

Dashnak Party, 79
Dhofar, 58, 62
Diem, Ngo Dinh, 80
Dien Bien Phu, 19, 50, 59
DPIK (Democratic Party of
    Iranian Kurdistan), 106

Egypt, 21, 25, 26, 108, 115, 119
El Salvador, 106
Entebbe, 98
EOKA (National Organization
    of Cypriot Struggle), 80
EPLF (Eritrean People's
    Liberation Front), 15, 51, 56,
    58, 93, 106
Eritrea, 15, 51, 61, 62, 93

Japan, 12, 19, 21–2, 27, 31, 33, 41, 43, 44–5, 57, 91, 92, 119
Japanese Red Army, 90, 101
Java, 39
JCAG (Justice Commandos for the Armenian Genocide), 95
Jena, 25
Jewish Defense League, 95
John Paul II, Pope, 84, 97, 113
Jordan, 15, 62, 82, 111, 123

Kabul, 63–4, 106
Karachi, 116
Kenya, 60
Khartoum, 61
Khomeini, Ayatollah Ruhollah, 93, 95, 98, 106, 109, 117
Khrushchev, Nikita, 108
Kitchener, Lord Herbert, 73
Komala, 106
Korea, 60, 108
Korea, North, 94
Kossuth, Lajos, 25
Kropotkin, Peter, 79
Kurdistan, Kurds, 15, 58, 62, 93, 106

Laqueur, Walter, 88
LARF (Lebanese Armed Revolutionary Factions), 100
Lawrence, T.E. (Lawrence of Arabia), 40
Le Bon, Gustave, 112
League of Nations, 32
Lebanon, 15, 82, 89, 92, 94, 95, 101, 111, 112, 116–23 *passim*
Lenin (Vladimir Ilich Ulyanov), 12, 28, 32, 42

Libya, 27, 40, 83, 93, 94, 96, 112, 116, 121–2
Lod, 90
London, 79, 98

Maalot, 92
MacArthur, Gen. Douglas, 22
Macedonians, 41, 79
Mahdists, 40
Makhno, Nestor, 41
Malaya, 13, 21, 30, 31, 60, 68, 72, 107
Malaysia, 120
Manchu dynasty/empire, 21, 26, 30
Manchuria, 20
Mao Zedong, 12, 30, 41, 42–4, 48, 50, 59
Marighella, Carlos; Marighella group, 82, 84–5, 86
Marseilles, 101
Marx, Karl, 79
Mau Mau, 60
Maxim, 40
Mazzini, Giuseppe, 25
McKinley, President William, 79
Mexico, 20, 41
Mikhailov, Ivan, 41
Milan, 103
Mogadishu, 98
Moluccans, 89
Mongolia, 41, 45
Montevideo, 85
Montoneros, 82, 102
Morenga, see South-West Africa
Moro, Aldo, 97
Morocco, 28, 30, 31, 71, 106
Moscow, 108